SOUTH WEST WAY

A WALKER'S GUIDE TO THE COAST PATH

BOOK 2

THE SOUTH COAST PENZANCE TO POOLE

Durlston Head

SOUTH WEST WAY

A WALKER'S GUIDE TO THE COAST PATH

BOOK 2

THE SOUTH COAST PENZANCE TO POOLE

Martin Collins

CICERONE PRESS

MILNTHORPE, CUMBRIA

ISBN 1 85284 026 9

For Diana and Paul who were with me constantly, in spirit if not in person, throughout the preparation of this guidebook.

All maps and photographs by the author

Front cover: St. Michael's Mount
Back Cover: Trewavas Head

Contents

PREFACE

Around the middle of the last century, coastal walking was starting to gain popularity but had not yet suffered the kind of access problems which were to blight the history of rambling in this country. Sir Leslie Stephen, an accomplished mountaineer and walker of the period, wrote about the south-west coast in his essay *In Praise of Walking*,

'...When you have made an early start, followed the coastguard track on the slopes above the cliffs, struggled through the gold and purple carpeting of gorse and heather on the moors, dipped down into quaint little coves with a primitive fishing village, followed by the blinding whiteness of the sands round a lonely bay, and at last emerged upon a headland where you can settle into a nook of the rocks, look down upon the glorious blue of the Atlantic waves breaking into foam on the granite, and see the distant sea-levels glimmering away until they blend imperceptably into cloudland; then you can consume your modest sandwiches, light your pipe, and feel more virtuous and thoroughly at peace with the universe than it is easy even to conceive yourself elsewhere...'

How times have changed! Following a journey by train and on foot around the British coast, Paul Theroux in his book *Kingdom by the Sea* writes,

'...the nuclear power stations and the junkyards and the shallys and sewage farms: you could do anything you liked on the British coast, beside the uncomplaining sea. The seaside belonged to everyone.'

His may be a sweeping and jaundiced view from which the south-west peninsula could claim exemption, yet it points up a national disregard for our coastal margins which could once be relied upon to cleanse man's poisons at each tidal surge.

Pollution by oil, coal waste, sewage, toxic heavy metals, radioactive emissions and agricultural run-off threatens not just the shoreline of Britain and other parts of Europe but the health of offshore waters too. As new incidents of cynical or accidental dumping come to light, misuse of the sea reaches scandalous proportions. Fishing techniques incorporating new technology are achieving catches beyond the dreams of traditional fishermen and in the process have upset for ever the balance between harvesting and regeneration.

Our coastal lands fare little better. Saltmarsh is 'reclaimed' for agriculture or building development, industrial plants smother the environment with fumes and dust, sand-dunes and fragile foreshores suffer degredation from plastic jetsam and overuse, while greater personal mobility increases pressure for ever more car parks, holiday camps and amenities.

The outlook can appear hopelessly bleak unless account is taken of the many agencies working in the opposite direction to exploitation. Prominent among them are the Nature Conservancy Council, the National Trust, the Countryside Commission, Greenpeace, Friends of the Earth, the Marine Conservation Society, the Royal Society for the Protection of Birds and numerous practical conservation groups. Their collective mission is helped by the establishment of Nature Reserves, Areas of Outstanding Natural Beauty and of course National Parks, bringing to the public's attention the need for positive action to protect vulnerable habitats.

For the most part, the south-west peninsula has been spared the worst examples of coastal and offshore pollution. Its stunningly beautiful coastline is a national asset of inestimable value - more scenically varied and richly endowed than almost anywhere else in Europe. Nature has healed the scars of 19th century mining and quarrying to a large degree, while the depopulation of once vigorous coastal communities, replaced by holiday and retirement homes, has tended to create stronger links between the coast and recreation than ever existed before. Water sports, sea-cliff climbing and walking all enjoy immense popularity alongside less demanding holiday pursuits which people of all ages and dispositions enjoy.

The National Trust continues to guard large tracts of our Heritage Coast against present and future abuse and the walker will encounter at first hand the Trust's good work in providing access and waymarking. Indeed it is the interested walker who best obtains an overview of our coastline's delights. Casual strollers will turn back half a mile from the nearest car park, few bothering to explore the cliffs and coves, valleys and beaches separating them from the next resort. Such secrets are the reward for a little enterprise! Only those who set out equipped to face the elements and a modicum of leg-work will discover the essential character of this primordial frontier where land meets ocean.

Whether your coastal journey is a modest jaunt or a long distance trek, you will surely gain new perspectives, a sharpening of the senses and a fuller appreciation of the interplay between nature and the hand of man.

WHY A GUIDEBOOK?

Announcing to a friend that I was preparing a guide to Britain's south-west peninsula coast path provoked a flippant response. 'Surely', he quipped, 'by simply keeping the sea to one side you wouldn't need a guide at all!'

He was correct in the narrow sense that it would be possible to walk 'blind' and to muddle through without going wildly astray. But enjoyable walking, however modest or ambitious its range, is not about muddling through or taking lines of least resistance and missing many worthwhile stretches of path in the process.

Like my friend, the uninitiated may be forgiven for imagining that a coast path simply follows the sea's edge. If it were so, a guidebook would indeed lose much of its *raison d'être*, but the reality is very far removed from this simplistic notion. There are many reasons why coastal walking creates demands for a guidebook. The picture is complex when viewed in terms of the south-west peninsula as a whole, not only because there are often more ways than one of getting from A to B, but because those ways themselves are subject to change.

The relentless, destructive force of waves breaking against the margin of land, exacerbated by the effects of rain and gales, produces a unique erosion problem for coast paths. Where cliffs of soft rock are undermined, the path line is brought closer and closer to the edge until it finally slips into the sea. Here and there, subsidence on a grand scale has completely redrawn coastal topography, but for the most part it is a lurking threat to farmland, sheep, cattle and property - a threat which the coastal walker ignores at his peril. A comparable loss of footpath metres per year, with all the associated re-routing and waymarking, never occurs on inland routes, however well walked.

New building development, changes in land use, military ranges and camps all constitute obstacles to progress necessitating detours or periodic re-routing of coast paths. River crossings and some stretches of beach walking require advance knowledge of tides, wading points and the location of footbridges or ferries.

Undertaken along the interface between land and ocean, coastal walking provides a level of interest unsurpassed by any other kind of pedestrian travel. Not only will you encounter rich and varied flora, seabird populations, marine life and a fascinating range of geological features, but the hand of man is also well represented. From Iron Age promontory fortifications to satellite tracking stations, from the relics of 19th century mining and quarrying to the latest automatic

An acorn signpost

lighthouses, from old fishing harbours to busy holiday resorts, man's industry punctuates the long unfolding passages of cliff and foreshore. It is to this wealth of detail, not just to route directions, that the guidebook author addresses himself.

Clear and consistent waymarking would help unravel the coast path's complexities, but standards vary from excellent to non-existent. On reflection, this is hardly surprising. Quite apart from changes - official and unofficial - which occur from time to time, signs and posts are subject to being installed wrongly (or worse still not at all), to vandalism, to becoming misaligned and to concealment in undergrowth. Furthermore, a sea mist or low cloud and driving rain will disorientate the coastal walker as effectively as the hill walker and the consequences of a wrong turn in the vicinity of dangrous ground are no different. Unfortunately, the path line on OS maps is often out of date owing to the rapidity with which changes take place.

I therefore make no apologies for providing detailed route notes, even if in fine conditions they appear to be stating the obvious. In poor visibility or adverse weather (contrary to tourist brochures, the south-west coast is not always bathed in sunshine!), knowing where you are and where to aim for can save endless frustration casting about for the correct path.

Even though fragments of information here and there may have already been overtaken by events at the time of going to press, routing changes are likely to be minor ones and should not affect the relevance of background material in the text. For the latest footpath update, buy a copy of the South West Way Association handbook, published each year. It is obtainable from bookshops in the south-west region, or through membership of the Association, which does sterling work in improving the coast path. To join, send name, address and £4 (couples £5) to: Mrs. M.Mcleod, Membership Secretary, South West Way Association, 1 Orchard Drive, Kingskerswell, Newton Abbot, Devon TQ12 5DG.

Prompted by the SWWA, the Countryside Commission and local authorities continue to negotiate a truly coastal footpath round our south-west peninsula. Intransigent landowners, industrial interests, bureaucratic apathy and the vagaries of erosion all conspire against the realisation of this ideal but, piece by piece and year by year, improvements are made. Meanwhile, good reader, I trust you will benefit a little from having your appetite whetted, your curiosity roused and your hiking made more enjoyable by the contents of this literary 'companion'.

MARTIN COLLINS
November 1988

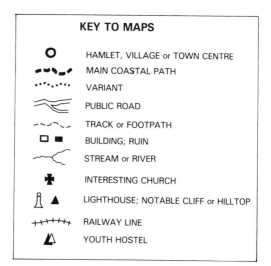

KEY TO MAPS

O	HAMLET, VILLAGE or TOWN CENTRE
	MAIN COASTAL PATH
	VARIANT
	PUBLIC ROAD
	TRACK or FOOTPATH
□ ■	BUILDING; RUIN
	STREAM or RIVER
✠	INTERESTING CHURCH
⌠ ▲	LIGHTHOUSE; NOTABLE CLIFF or HILLTOP
+++++	RAILWAY LINE
◭	YOUTH HOSTEL

ORIGINS AND DEVELOPMENT OF COASTAL PATHS

No doubt a few stretches of our coastal footpaths date back thousands of years. Mesolithic man, who foraged for shellfish and collected flints from pebble beaches to fashion arrowheads for hunting, would have worn the first narrow trods - some widened by centuries of use, many lost to the relentless march of erosion, buried by the plough or obliterated beneath building development.

Far more paths owe their existence to fishing and the need for communities to launch and beach their craft in various states of tides and weather, as well as gaining access to coves, headlands and neighbouring villages. Even so, long expanses of cliff and strand would rarely have seen a human visitor. Certainly there was no concept of 'holidaymaking' until the 19th century when an expanding railway network heralded the era of mass tourism for an increasingly industrial society. Until then, life for the common man on land adjacent to the coast would have been subject to the vagaries of climate and to the rigours of fishing or agriculture. Little time, energy or inclination would have remained to undertake travel for its own sake.

Later, more tracks and pathways would evolve in certain areas as coastal industries such as mining and quarrying began to flourish. The construction of harbours not only facilitated the import-export of industrial materials but also encouraged trade in commodities of all kinds. Before the advent of railway transport, ports large and small played vital roles in the nation's economy.

We can assume that more and more shoreline became familiar to these coastal inhabitants as they fished, laid nets, gathered seafood, plants and herbs, followed ships in distress and searched for survivors or valuable wreckage - in addition to the to-ing and fro-ing of everyday life.

However, by far the most significant factor in the evolution of our present coastal footpaths took place early in the 18th century, when the government of the day imposed heavy customs duties on imported luxury goods - especially wines and spirits - in order to generate much needed revenue. Fishing communities, quick to seize an opportunity to raise their living above subsistence level, turned to smuggling. Using their intimate knowledge of sea and coastline, fishermen and their fellow conspirators inland openly flaunted the law and created a thriving 'black economy', particularly along the south coast of

England. Indeed, even by 1724, Daniel Defoe had been moved to declare, '...that smuggling and roguing...is the reigning commerce of all this part of the English coast, from the mouth of the Thames to Land's End.

So seriously did it come to regard this lawlessness that in 1736 Parliament introduced an Act laying down severe penalties, including whipping and hard labour, for anyone found within 5 miles of the sea who could not satisfy the authorities that they had good reason to be there. The Act remained in force for almost a century and, of course, deterred any significant development of coastal walking and exploration for pleasure during that time.

Owing to elevated levels of duty, profits to be made from smuggling were considerable and it became widespread and highly organised, especially in the south-east where continental Europe is closest. No responsible government could tolerate this state of affairs indefinitely. Around 1815, a nightly shore patrol of the Kent and Sussex coast by sailors was set up. This was soon followed by the inauguration of the Coastguard Service in 1822, whereafter the entire coastline of the British Isles was regularly patrolled and coastal footpaths as we know them today became established.

Nearest the French coast, coastguards were stationed at 100 yard intervals (an astonishingly heavy deployment), while farther west and north each officer would cover from ½ to 3 or 4 miles. Coastguards were universally unpopular people, seen by the local communities as denying them access to a little luxury in otherwise extremely hard times. Not surprisingly, villagers refused to lodge officers in their houses, so specially designed stations were constructed with an eye to protecting their occupants from a hostile populace.

Conditions of service were rigorous. Duty hours, mostly at night, were long, to be worked in all weathers, over hazardous terrain and always carrying the added risk of encountering a determined band of smugglers. Coastguards were armed and initially there were some violent confrontations, resulting in injury and death on both sides; eventually, however, the rule of law prevailed and smuggling dwindled to a small-scale operation.

By the mid-1850's, the government's conversion to the principles of free trade had brought about dramatic reductions in tariffs and associated duties, so that contraband was no longer as profitable as it had once been and coastguard manning levels were reduced accordingly. Over the ensuing years, the Coastguard Service has shifted its attention to safeguarding the passage of shipping and co-ordinating rescue for those in difficulty on the coast itself or offshore.

Sadly, many lookout posts are now abandoned, boarded up or at the mercy of the elements. Footpaths, however, are far more durable in the long term and it is largely thanks to those early coastguard patrols that we have a South West Way today.

A BRIEF HISTORY OF THE SOUTH WEST WAY

The first dispute concerning access to the coast took place at Exeter Assizes as far back as 1838, when smuggling was still rife. John Ames, described as 'a gentleman of large fortune' had erected a wall around his recently acquired estate west of Lyme Regis, blocking off the coast path which had been in common use by locals for decades, if not centuries. All attempts at persuasion failed, so the local people took Ames to court - and won their case.

The outcome of such disputes were not always to be as happy as this however, although until the middle of the 19th century coastal walking would have been virtually hindrance-free, providing one had a convincing line to offer the coastguard! But as seaside resorts sprouted and improving transport began to feed visitors in increasing numbers to coastal locations, problems arose with inappropriate behaviour and abuse of the environment: in those days there was no country code!

So, uneducated in the need for a responsible attitude towards natural habitats, some visitors made nuisances of themselves and antagonised landowners. Measures were taken along the North Devon coast -notably at Clovelly, Lynton and Ilfracombe - to restrict public access to the cliffs by imposing admission tolls, erecting gates and fences or even closing off sections altogether. As can be imagined, such actions triggered considerable controversy, bringing into sharp focus the whole debate on recreational rights of way.

All our Long Distance Footpaths have had to be negotiated, piece by piece, with sometimes obstinate landowners; the South West Way, still technically incomplete as a continuous coastal footpath, is no exception.

By the beginning of this century, judges presiding over access disputes were still ruling in favour of landowners and against rights of way for purposes of pleasure or intellectual interest, however ancient the usage of such paths. Walking organisations were in their infancy and no match for their wealthy adversaries, whether landowning gentry or the new breed of property developers cashing in on the growth of seaside resorts. In 1932 the Rights of Way Act helped clarify

13

the situation, while the Access to Mountains Bill of 1939 raised genuine hopes that mountain, moor, heath, cliff and downland would become more widely available to the general public. Ministerial interpretation of the access clauses and a tightening of the trespass laws, however, slammed the door in the face of the access movement and no improvements materialised.

First official interest in the notion of a South West Way came in a report by a government committee in 1941 under Lord Chief Justice Scott, set up to look at problems of rural land use and the establishment of National Parks. It was not until 1947, however, that a Town and Country Planning Act specifically froze development on the coast with no obligation to pay compensation. In the same year a government report specifically recommended the making of a coast path around the south-west peninsula, noting that over ⅓ of the Cornish coast was not open to the walker and that a total of almost 100 miles of extra footpath would be necessary to create a continuous route.

The appearance of the National Parks Commission (now the Countryside Commission) in 1949 did not produce instant progress, but eventually a South West Coastal Path was plotted out. Unfortunately, the Commission failed to use its teeth, taking the line of least resistance when confronted by an obstructive landowner - to the great detriment of the path which was routed unnecessarily and unsatisfactorily inland at such locations. More happily, the National Trust inaugurated its Enterprise Neptune project in May 1965 and has been acquiring sections of coastline for the nation's heritage ever since. The official opening of the Cornwall coast path took place in May 1973 at Newquay, and of the 'complete' South West Way (still technically unfinished) 5 years later. Many stretches remain which stray from the coast for one reason or another, despite the recommendations of 4 government reports. Each year some progress is made towards achieving the ultimate objective of a continuous and genuinely coastal footpath - a mile of new path here, a re-routing there or the removal of obstructions.

The South West Way Association

The Association was formed in the early 1970's when the idea of a long-distance footpath round the south-west coast was being implemented; those involved believed that little was being done on the South West Way which, in their opinion, was potentially a very fine footpath indeed. The objects of the Association are to secure the protection and preservation of an acceptable south-west coastal path and public access to that path. They provide a forum in which different interests connected with the path and its use can discuss problems of mutual concern.

They continually prod the authorities to complete the path and to see that it is properly waymarked and maintained, and are in constant communication with the Countryside Commission, the National Trust, the Exmoor National Park Authority and the four County Councils - Somerset, Devon, Cornwall and Dorset.

The Association disseminates information on the coast path to members of the public and produces an annual handbook which is sent free to members. This contains details of accommodation, a book list, rail and bus services, ferries and tide tables, as well as an update on the state of the path which undergoes minor changes from year to year.

Requests for membership should be sent to Mrs. M.Mcleod, 1 Orchard Drive, Kingkerswell, Newton Abbot, Devon TQ12 5DG; tel (08047) 3061. Or to the Secretary - Mr. E.Wallis, 'Windlestraw', Penquit, Ermington, Nr. Ivybridge, Devon; tel (0752) 896237.

ABOUT COASTAL WALKING

The South West Way comprises many footpath segments linked together into a virtually continuous right of way. It stretches some 567 miles (912km) from Minehead in north Somerset to South Haven Point near Poole in Dorset and incorporates the Somerset and North Devon, North Cornwall, South Cornwall, South Devon and Dorset coast paths.

Although some sections of path are autonomous, with their own individual characteristics, a long-distance walker tackling stages of several days' or weeks' duration will tread the entire gamut of underfoot conditions reflecting an enormous variety of geographical features and terrain. High clifftop, sand and pebbly beaches, dismantled railway, woodland, estuary shore, grassy hillside, sand dunes, riverbank, country lane, farm track and urban pavement all bear the generic title 'coast path'.

A facet of coastal walking in the south-west absent from much (though not all) of Britain's hill country concerns the relative proximity of road, farmstead or settlement. Indeed, some stretches of path, more especially on the south coast, are little more than contiguous urban seafront owing to the density of resort development in sheltered locations such as Torbay.

There is no real contradiction, however, in stating that a great deal of coastal walking is wild and remote. Between villages or resorts, access inland may not exist, sometimes for many miles. Only in emergency would the crossing of hedges, walls, steep or impenetrable undergrowth etc. be justified to obtain help. You are travelling in a largely unusable corridor between sea and terra firma, barely beyond the waves and spray of high tides - an unstable mini-wilderness where the ocean's awesome and hypnotic presence is keenly felt.

Except in sparsely populated areas, farms and villages just inland sometimes offer hospitality of one kind or another - cream teas, camping, the occasional pub or bed and breakfast - but are reached only by time consuming detours. A fairly regular succession of amenities actually on the coast allows you to plan a day's hike around halts for meals and drinks, but the intervening miles do need the same careful consideration as their hill-country equivalents with regard to weather, distances, fitness, daylight hours etc.

Substantial parts of the coast path run along the perimeter of farmland - often rough pasture or cultivated fields - but the nature of walking on that perimeter depends upon underlying geology, steepness and accessibility, and exposure to prevailing weather. In places you are held tightly between field fence and cliff edge, elsewhere you will be traversing rugged hillsides through gorse and thorn bushes or dense woodland.

By high summer, undergrowth on sheltered sections threatens to overwhelm the path. A thin scattering of local council employees, often with individual responsibility for many miles of footpath, use petrol-driven 'strimmers' to keep the way open, turning their hand to repairing stiles, gates and fences during the winter.

Gradients can be very steep, but with a few exceptions are less sustained than in mountain country. There are, however, more ups and downs per mile on average as the path dips to cove or beach before rising to the next clifftop. Owing to this frequency of ascent and descent, coastal walking is no 'easy option' and even hardened hill walkers can be surprised by the demands it makes on energy and overall fitness. Some sections are exceptionally easy on the legs and lungs, while others will challenge the fittest, but most fall into an intermediate category which leaves the walker comfortable enough to enjoy his surroundings.

Waymarking and path maintenance are carried out by local authorities (except in the Exmoor National Park), who receive full grant aid from central government and thus incur no charge on local communities for this work. Unfortunately not all authorities honour their obligations and while standards are perceptibly improving in line

Black Head (distant right) from Polrudden Cliffs

with increasing public interest in coast path walking, omissions and neglect can be expected here and there. In general, the situation seems best adjacent to popular tourist areas where casual walking is undertaken by holidaymakers who expect paths to be clear and well signed (this does not include urban shoreline where a coast path, as such, is often non-existent). On wilder and remote parts of the coastline, conditions and waymarking can be less than satisfactory, though only the more experienced and resourceful walker is likely to reach there in the first place. Wherever the path crosses National Trust property, waymarking and standards of maintenance are usually impeccable.

A final word of warning about erosion and subsidence. I was lucky to escape with my life while researching for this book when the cliff edge at Cleave, near Crackington Haven on the north coast of Cornwall, disappeared in front of my feet, taking several metres of path with it. Two walkers ahead, approaching from the opposite direction, had seen the slippage starting and kept well back. My companion and I had no way of knowing the path was about to collapse and had we been there 5 seconds earlier would have been swept down to our certain deaths. I mention this incident not to scaremonger but to underline the need for vigilance, particularly after periods of very wet or windy weather.

The old coastguard paths have survived for well over a century, but it is a measure of the sea's power that man is in constant retreat. Softer rocks and shales are first to succumb and the walker is advised to take note of local geology; the granites and serpentine of the far south-west are more resistant to erosion. Watch carefully for overhangs, cracks and hollows and be extra cautious wherever the path runs close to the edge.

Red lifebelts and rescue kits - even emergency telephones - are installed at obviously hazardous locations. These are useful in certain situations (eg. rock-climbing accidents, getting into difficulties swimming or being cut off by the tide), but the kind of risks which threaten walkers are much more universal and cannot be safeguarded against except by attitude of mind and taking sensible precautions. In the event of an accident, contact the police who will, in turn, inform HM Coastguard and the relevant emergency services.

Finally, when best to go? May and June are favoured months in an average year, characterised by prolific wild flowers, freedom from undergrowth, long hours of daylight, usually good weather and an absence of holiday crowds. However, September and October can be equally fine. During both spring and autumn there is less pressure on accommodation, access to the coast and parking space, as well as on other amenities.

PUBLIC TRANSPORT

British Rail's main inter-city line from London, the Midlands and the North runs through Taunton, Exeter and Plymouth to Penzance, its southern terminus. Trains are frequent, fast and some provide sleeping car accommodation, but reservations for all seats are necessary on busy summer weekends. The following notes will indicate how to reach the coast path from railway stations, but more detailed enquiries will be needed to ascertain exact connections. Some branch lines operate in the summer months only.

Coast Path at	BR Station
PENZANCE	Main line terminus
FALMOUTH	Change at Truro
PAR	Main line station
LOOE	Change at Liskeard

PLYMOUTH	Main line station
PAIGNTON	Change at Newton Abbot
TORQUAY	Change at Newton Abbot
TEIGNMOUTH,	
DAWLISH,	
DAWLISH	
WARREN	
and STARCROSS	Change at Exeter
EXMOUTH	Change at Exeter
SIDMOUTH	Honiton then bus
SEATON/LYME	
REGIS	Axminster then bus
WEYMOUTH	Main line station
POOLE	Main line station

As an often less expensive long-distance alternative, National Express coaches operate from cities and towns all over the country to the south-west, for connection with local buses. For details contact your local National Express office or travel agent.

Bus travel in the south-west, as elsewhere in Britain, has undergone major transformation since deregulation. Some services have improved but in other areas remain patchy or non-existent. For the occasional bus ride, call at or phone the nearest Tourist Information Office (see 'Useful Addresses'); if, however, you require timetables for planning, consult the South West Way Association's annual handbook which lists bus operators, or write to the address below: Western National at National House, Queen Street, Exeter EX4 3TF (stating which area you need timetables for).

A book containing timetables for all public transport in Cornwall (bus, coach, rail, ferries and air) is available from Cornwall County Council, County Hall, Truro, tel: (0872) 74282 (weekdays).

Many more points on the coast path can be reached by using combinations of train, coach and bus. It is worth bearing in mind that winter services are less frequent and may need to be augmented by taxi, private car or even hitching if access to or from remote locations is sought.

ACCOMMODATION - CAMPING, YOUTH HOSTELS, BED AND BREAKFAST

This chapter will be of greater interest to long-distance walkers who need to plan ahead than to those undertaking day walks from a central base, although all coastal walkers will benefit from knowing what to expect along the way.

Approaches to travelling on foot vary from the backpacker who carries a lightweight tent and equipment and seeks out each night 'wild' pitches in lonely places, to the patroniser of luxury hotels and restaurants. Between these extreme ends of the spectrum lie the bed-and-breakfaster, the youth hosteller and those who combine various forms of accommodation according to circumstances.

Owing to the remote nature of parts of the south coast, lightweight camping is a real option and gives the backpacking walker maximum flexibility over where to end the day. However, camping is not without problems of its own. Campsites *per se* are relatively thin on the ground in some areas, tend to open only in the summer and are not necessarily conducive to a restful night's sleep! (A list of campsites is issued to members of the Camping and Caravanning Club of Great Britain, 11 Grosvenor Place, London SW1W 0EY.) Some stretches are simply too built up for camping to be feasible except on sites, which are rarely close to the coast path itself.

Genuine backpackers able to cope with a minimum or complete absence of facilities can ask at farms adjacent to the coast (individuals or couples only - no large groups). Farmers are nearly always friendly and sympathetic, but **never** pitch on farmland without asking permission first. You will be able to obtain fresh water, possibly milk too, but once in the field you are shown to, you are on your own. Always offer to pay for the pitch, even if payment is sometimes refused: this maintains goodwill and smooths the way for future lightweight campers.

Finding true 'wild' pitches is possible for experienced backpackers who know what to look for. Much depends on wind strength and direction (actual and expected), for there is little shelter from an onshore blow. Most promising locations are stream valleys and the tops of beaches. Pure water is not easy to come by as streams often flow through farms and pasture on their way to the sea; springs, however, are usually clear and are marked on OS 1:25,000 maps. If in doubt, either use purifying tablets or be prepared to carry water from the last reliable source.

You will pass numerous wild pitches which are too close to habitations to use. Discretion and sensitivity to other path users are essential in choosing a pitch - remember that large sections of path run through designated Areas of Outstanding Natural Beauty or Heritage Coast. The National Trust does not allow camping on its land nor on its farms.

The backpacker's code of leaving no trace of an overnight pitch assumes extra significance on a coastal route where others will pass by after you. However, it is a style of travel which offers independence and close contact with the environment; furthermore, when combined with camping at farms and official sites, accommodation costs are reduced to their lowest level.

Apart from an inherent lack of home comforts such as hot baths and clean sheets, camping's main disadvantage is the need to carry a heavier rucksack. This imposes additional strain on the feet and joints and turns hilly stages into altogether more strenuous propositions. The best advice is to keep rucksack weight as light as possible and to make one or two 'dry runs' near home to familiarise yourself with the backpacking process.

Youth hostels are situated at Penzance, Coverack, Falmouth, Boswinger (near Dodman Point), Fowey, Plymouth, Salcombe, Strete, Torbay, Beer, Bridport (inland), Litton Cheney (inland), Lulworth Cove and Swanage,(for details see 'Useful Addresses'). Of course, these are too few for long-distance walkers to rely on exclusively but used in conjunction with bed and breakfast or camping, youth hostels provide cheap and convivial overnight halts. Individual hostels, often in marvellous settings, could be used as a base for 2 or 3 nights' stay, enabling expeditions to be made along the coast path in both directions.

For details of south coast hostels and application forms, write to the YHA Area Office, Belmont Place, Stoke, Plymouth; tel: (0752) 562753. Advance booking is necessary during the busy summer months, but it is worth remembering that there is no upper age limit for members and that motorised transport can be used. For membership, write to the YHA, St. Albans, Herts. AL1 2DY.

Bed and breakfast establishments will be found in abundance at villages and towns along the coast path or a short distance off it. There are substantial sectors of path however, which are devoid of any human settlement and it is there that accommodation problems can arise. When arriving at a town with a Tourist Information Office, staff will happily assist in finding you a bed for the night, but if you require the security of advance bookings, more organised planning will have to be done. In their annual handbook, the South West Way Association publishes a list of recommended bed and breakfast places, including phone numbers and prices; holiday accommodation books obtainable from newsagents will also yield helpful information.

In the author's experience it is quite unnecessary to reserve accommodation except during the school holiday period and perhaps a fortnight either side. If it is imperative to book a sequence of bed and breakfasts in advance, err on the side of underestimating daily mileage. Adverse weather, injury, fatigue or an unforeseen delay can interrupt the journey and set you on a gruelling treadmill from which it is hard to escape. Far better to keep in hand time and energy with which to enjoy each day's destination.

Most guest-house proprietors, innkeepers and hoteliers on or near the coast path will do what they can to dry out wet gear and satisfy healthy appetites. Many will provide packed lunches on request and walkers are assured of a comfortable night's rest away from the elements, though it is not always easy to make an early start.

OBTAINING SUPPLIES AND REFRESHMENTS

With the exception of a few stretches of remote and uninhabited coast, there is usually no difficulty in buying food along the path - even tiny hamlets often boast a Post Office/General Store. It is wise to carry rations for unexpected delays however, as well as extra energy food (fruit, chocolate etc.) to help you deal with more strenuous terrain. Only in two or three areas along the south coast are you more than a couple of hours' walk from a place of refreshment, whether it be pub, cafe, hotel, restaurant, kiosk or shop. At the season's height, some strength of will is required to resist the coffees, pub lunches, cream teas and ice-creams which seem to beckon on all sides!

It is vital to realise, however, that many such fleshpots are seasonal. Walkers setting out in months other than May to September will encounter a vastly restricted choice. Indeed, long-distance winter expeditions present considerable logistical problems, even though generally milder weather in the south-west is more favourable for hiking than conditions in hill country further north.

Banks can be few and far between and minor branches often open only one or two days per week. Credit cards may be acceptable in larger guest-houses, hotels and restaurants, but payment for goods and services must otherwise be paid for by cash or cheque. It is certainly prudent to carry plenty of cash or use a Girobank account - Post Offices are more common and are open longer hours.

CLOTHING AND EQUIPMENT

For the majority of coastal walkers who set out during the months of longer daylight hours and warmer conditions from April to October, a balance has to be struck between hiking comfort and protection from the elements. Even in high summer it may be wet and windy at times and can feel unseasonably chilly. Then shell clothing (preferably breathable) over a light shirt and shorts will often suffice while on the move, with a jumper and lightweight trousers to slip on when you stop. In early spring or autumn, a thicker shirt, extra sweater or pile jacket, woolly hat and breeches or windproof trousers may be needed.

Burning ultra-violet radiation from summer sunshine is accentuated on the coast by reflection off the sea and sand. Tempting though it may be to wear very little on such glorious days, you are just as vulnerable to sunburn as beachgoers. Shoulders, arm tops, foreheads, nose and fronts of legs can become painfully burned while the preoccupations of the route hold your attention: good advice is to avoid sleeveless garments, to wear a brimmed sunhat and light, loose clothing. Applying a high-factor suncream to exposed skin is a wise precaution, especially for fair skinned people or those unaccustomed to bright sunshine.

A heat wave may be the holidaymaker's dream but can produce gruelling conditions for walkers. When you are hot, thirsty and tired, sunshine becomes as much the enemy as cold is in winter. There is precious little shade along the coast path and although good for splashing over yourself, stream water is not usually safe to drink. Unless you know there are refreshment points on route, always carry some fresh water in hot weather.

Sunlight can be dazzling when walking - a pair of polarizing sunglasses will relieve your eyes of strain and cut out specular reflections on the sea, allowing you to look through its surface as an added bonus.

Needless to say, carrying a change of clothes in the rucksack is essential if you are planning a walk of several days duration or longer. Clothing can get as damp from perspiration as from rain and with the physical effort of walking will soon need washing! Hikers using hostels or guest-houses may need to be more fastidious than campers who have only themselves for company and can afford to wait a day or two for their next shower! A swimming costume and towel will open up possibilities for bathing when the opportunity arises.

It is assumed that backpackers know what gear to take along so this will not be dealt with here. Any additional items to include can be ascertained from these introductory chapters. Camping Gaz, methylated spirit or paraffin wax for stoves are only obtainable in larger towns or well appointed campsites, as are water purifying tablets, photographic film and batteries and other articles of a specialised nature.

Rucksacks are important pieces of equipment, not just for the backpacker whose 'mobile home' they contain, but for the hosteller and bed-and-breakfaster too. Spare clothing, cagoule and overtrousers, food, water, first aid kit (including telephone coins, and emergency whistle), toilet gear, books, camera and film, maps, compass and guidebook will all sometimes need to be packed away, especially in wet weather when a number of plastic bags will ensure everything is kept dry. Add a torch for off-season hiking.

Rucksack weight above about 12lbs. (5kg) is carried more comfortably when a flexible lightweight frame or insert and a hip belt are built into the pack design. Such features spread the load, provide contour rigidity against the back and aid postural stability when climbing stiles or rocks, particularly in a wind. Straps allowing potentially wet and muddy items to be attached externally are useful. Even day walkers will need a robust, if smaller, pack for long or uninhabited stretches or for out-of-season hiking.

Binoculars or a monocular will bring a good deal of pleasure, not only from viewing along the coast but providing close-ups of seabirds, seals, shipping and inaccessible shoreline. If your camera will take filters, be sure to use a UV eliminator which doubles as protection from salt spray. A polarizer will add depth to colour shots and give you sometimes surprising glimpses of what lies underwater. A pocket-sized radio is useful for obtaining weather and shipping forecasts as well as for entertainment and news if backpacking, but as with all such non-essentials, personal preferences and accumulative pack weight will be the arbitrators.

Finally footwear - for a number of reasons not as straightforward a subject as one might imagine! The author has met long-distance backpackers who made do with trainers and has himself used them successfully at times. They have three main drawbacks however, which detract from their advantages of comfort, light weight and low cost.

First they offer no ankle support and this cannot be ignored as much of the going is rough, sometimes steep and often requires accurate foot placement. Carrying a heavy pack simply exacerbates the problem. Second, few trainers possess soles suitable for gripping on loose slopes. Although cleated rubber soles as fitted to boots also fail to provide traction on smooth, wet surfaces, trainers give little 'bite' in mud or wet grass either. Third, you will get wet feet very quickly -from rain certainly, but more commonly from moisture-laden grasses and undergrowth which in summer curl over the path, obscuring its surface and acting as a continuous footbath! In such conditions, it has to be said, leather boots too will become saturated although with help from gaiters or anklets the process is retarded.

In their favour, trainers are ideal for easy sections of path in dry weather and in accommodation or when eating out. Having once become wet, they do dry out faster than boots.

Heavy walking boots are generally considered unnecessary for any kind of rough walking unless cold and the wearing of crampons are likely factors. Probably the best footwear for the South West Way are lightweight leather boots with good tread depth, ankle support and well waxed for maximum water resistance. Two pairs of socks will help prevent blisters, but at the end of the day the only guarantee of foot comfort is previous mileage to harden feet and break in boots.

MAPS, TIDES AND RIVER CROSSINGS

This guidebook covers the south coast path and its variants in considerable detail but there remains a strong case for supplementing its use with Ordnance Survey maps. A compass weighs next to nothing and will rarely be needed, but the author has found one useful on a few occasions when a sudden sea mist rolled in or it was necessary to navigate off route on little used rights of way.

1:50,000 scale maps are perfectly adequate for walking on the south-west coast, though bear in mind that the path line may have changed here and there since the last revision or may not be marked at all. 1:25,000 scale maps show a wealth of detail and are especially valuable to those interested in archaeological or industrial remains: there are rather too many sheets involved for the longer-distance walker to carry.

1:50,000 Landranger maps required for the south coast are (in walk order):

No.	Title
203	Land's End and the Lizard
204	Truro and Falmouth
200	Newquay and Bodmin
201	Plymouth and Launceston
202	Torbay and South Dartmoor

192	Exeter and Sidmouth
193	Taunton and Lyme Regis
194	Dorchester and Weymouth
195	Bournemouth and Purbeck

1:25,000 Pathfinder maps (First or Second Series) available for the south coast are (in path order):

No.	*Title*
SW 52/62	Helston and Prussia Cove
SW 61/71	Lizard Point
SW 72/82	Helford River
SW 83	Falmouth and St.Mawes
SW 94 ⎫ SX 04 ⎭	Mevagissey and Tregory
SX 05/15	St.Austell and Fowey
SX 25/35	Looe
SX 45/55	Plymouth
SX 54/64	Newton Ferrers and Bigbury
SX 73	Salcombe
SX 74/84	Kingsbridge
SX 85/95	Dartmouth and Brixham
SX 86/96	Torbay
SX 87/97	Newton Abbot and Teignmouth
SY 08/18	Sidmouth
SY 29/39	Lyme Regis
SY 49/59	Bridport
SY 58	Abbotsbury
SY 68/78	Weymouth North
SY 67/77	Weymouth
SY 88/98	Wareham
SY 87/97 ⎫ SZ 07 ⎭	Purbeck
SZ 08	Studland

The ebb and flow of tides will rarely escape your notice while walking on the coast path. For the most part, this diurnal cycle is of incidental interest, determining whether or not the foreshore rocks and beaches are exposed and accessible. In at least two situations, however, tides assume greater significance for the coastal walker.

One of these is where the route or a desirable alternative takes to the beach: especially if this entails walking beneath high cliffs, there is a real danger of becoming cut off by a rising tide. Many such incidents involving unwary holidaymakers occur each year and although the

Waiting for the ferry to Kingswear

outcome is usually a happy one, perhaps following rescue by rope or·
helicopter, fatalities do happen.

It goes without saying that to embark upon a lengthy beach walk
without prior knowledge of escape routes or times of low and high
water is asking for trouble. Raising the alarm is extremely difficult
from the base of cliffs and lone walkers are at a further disadvantage if
climbing to safety is the only option.

Freak waves of greater height than average occuring at unpredictable intervals are an added hazard to beware of when scrambling or
walking close to the sea's edge. Lives are lost with depressing regular-
ity, not always from conscious risk taking but through a lack of understanding of how the ocean behaves.

The other occasion when tide times become vital to the walker
concerns the crossing of river mouths by wading or ferry. On the
north coast, only the River Gannel at Newquay can be negotiated on
foot but along the south coast, river crossings are more frequent.

Reference to route notes in this guidebook provides all the relevant information on ferries wherever they occur along the coast path. Some are seasonal, others only operate each side of high water, others still are year-round and run at regular intervals from early till late. Low water can affect the embarkation and landing points of ferries and one should always be prepared to adopt an alternative strategy if for one reason or another the ferry should not be running.

Wading a river mouth is not always as simple as it sounds. After periods of rain and during the tide cycle except at low water, the channel may be too deep and the current too swift for safe human passage. In fact, crossing the River Erme, where no ferry exists, and some other rivers outside the main holiday season can involve walkers in lengthy delays. Recourse to tide tables rather than casual observation is recommended to establish times of high and low water, though potential delay to walkers on the north coast will be minimal compared to that on the south coast. Tide tables are available from many newsagents and bookshops in the south-west, while the South West Way Association publish figures for the rivers Erme and Avon in their annual handbook (see 'Useful Addresses'). Tide times are also often displayed at seafronts and harbours.

WEATHER

Over a half of Cornwall is situated less than 5 miles (8km) from the sea and even central Devon locations are only some 18 miles (30km) distant. This proximity to vast expanses of open water on 3 sides differentiates the climate of the south-west peninsula from that of the rest of Britain. One effect is to reduce both seasonal and diurnal variations in temperature so that there is less fluctuation than further up the mainland. Along the south coast of Cornwall and Devon, the average mean temperature is 11°C - a little lower towards the south-east of Devon and into Dorset.

June is usually the sunniest month, December the dullest and there is more winter daylight than anywhere else in Britain. In the extreme south-west, around 1,750 sunshine hours per year can be expected; taking the year as a whole, this is the country's warmest spot, along with the Isles of Scilly, the Channel Isles and Isle of Wight.

Sea temperatures are lowest in late February/early March but January is normally the area's coldest month, with average means of between zero and 2.5°C. Lowest recorded temperatures around the coast itself rarely exceed −12°C.

July is the warmest month, with mean maxima of 19 to 22°C

(usually reached in mid-afternoon), though the relatively cold sea prevents the coast itself from becoming quite as warm as inland. The highest regional temperature in recent years - 33.9°C - was recorded to the east at Southampton during 1976 the 'Year of the Drought'.

Relative humidity - on average around 85% - is higher in winter and at night, though during heavy fog or persistent rain it can reach 100%. Rainfall for the region varies between 1,200mm (47in.) and 800m (31in.) per annum - November, December and January being wettest, April and June driest. Heavy downpours associated with thunderstorms can occur anytime but mainly over the land in summer and over a warmer sea in winter. The sea's presence produces a more uniform incidence of thunderstorms throughout the year than farther into the mainland where they occur principally during the summer. (Walkers should take care not to linger on high, open clifftops during thunderstorms owing to the chance of lightning strike.)

Snowfall is rarer here than elsewhere in Britain and usually falls on 10 or less days a year around the coast, while most coastal locations see a ground frost on between 35 and 60 days.

Sea (or 'advection') fog forms when moist, warm air is in contact with a relatively cold sea surface. It is most frequent in spring and early summer along the coast itself and immediately inland. Months most affected by sea fogs in the south-west peninsula are June and July.

Because Atlantic depressions are more frequent in winter, winds then are usually strongest. As one would expect on such an exposed peninsula, south-westerly gales are more commonly experienced than in the rest of England. The extreme south-west of Cornwall can expect 25 or more gale days per year when mean wind speeds exceed 34 knots over any 10 minute period. Gale days decrease as you move inland and north-east. Extreme wind speeds occasionally occur, such as 91 knots recorded at the Lizard, in south-west Cornwall, on 15th January 1979 - not the sort of weather for a cliff path walk!

In fact, wind speed and direction is of particular concern to walkers as it can hinder progress on coast paths more seriously than any other single factor. Wind speed is assessed visually by the Beaufort Scale, an international standard for mariners which can be of considerable interest to coastal walkers, particularly in conjuction with broadcast shipping forecasts.

Weather forecasts are provided by national BBC radio and television, as well as by the press, and will provide general indications to the expected weather countrywide. However, as with all geographically unique regions, parts of the south-west peninsula often create

Beaufort No.	Designation/average speed in knots	Effects of wind on the sea
0	Calm - under 1	Smooth, glassy sea.
1	Light - 2	Small, scale-like ripples without crests.
2	Light - 5	Small waves, still short and smooth but more pronounced.
3	Light - 8	White caps forming but still mostly smooth. Occasional white foam appearing.
4	Moderate - 13	Waves still small but longer. White caps fairly general.
5	Fresh - 18	Moderate-sized waves now long and more pronounced. White caps everywhere. Occasional spray forming.
6	Strong - 24	Formation of larger waves. Crests break and leave areas of white foam. Some spray.
7	Strong - 30	Sea heaps up. Long streaks of foam begin to form along the wind direction. More spray. (Some difficulty walking against the wind.)
8	Gale - 37	Large waves with very long crests. Spray blown off wave crests. Long, thick streaks of foam. (Walking progress considerably impeded.)
9	Severe gale - 44	Mountainous seas. Dense streaks of foam along direction of wind. Wave crests begin to topple and roll over. Spray may affect visibility.
10	Storm - 52	Towering, tumbling waves with long, overhanging crests. Sea white with foam. Visibility restricted by spray. (Considerable structural damage on land.)
11	Violent storm - 60	Extremely mountainous sea, white and foaming. Drastically reduced visibility. (Widespread damage on land.)
12	Hurricane - 68 +	Air filled with driving foam and spray as wave crests are torn off by the wind. Sea completely white and frothy. Visibility very difficult. (Devastating damage on land but rarely experienced.)

local climates of their own, much to the chagrin of the tourist industry which stands to lose custom from adverse weather forecasts which tend to tar large areas with the same brush!

Forecasts on local radio and television are more reliable and the BBC Shipping Forecasts at 1.55pm. and 5.50pm. are especially useful if you are already familiar with meteorological terminology; sea areas Portland and Plymouth are relevant to the south coast. Weather forecasts for the south-west may also be obtained by telephoning (0898) 600291; (0898) 500481; or (0898) 333598.

HOW TO USE THIS GUIDE

The tradition of walking the south-west coast path in an anti-clock-wise direction springs from there being more miles in total with wind and weather behind you than against you. Expeditions on the north coast alone, however - rather less than half the path's overall distance of 567 miles - gain little from this tradition as the predominant direction of travel faces south-west. Nevertheless, waymarking tends to favour the anti-clockwise walker, who in any case will probably prefer a more north-easterly starting point for a long-distance trek in order to reduce initial journey time from other parts of the country. The picture is reversed of course for long-distance walkers starting the southern half of the route from Penzance! (For details of walking on the North Coast, see this guidebook's sister volume - *Minehead to Penzance*.)

Attempting to describe the path in both directions at once would be unwieldy to say the least, so the author has adopted an anti-clockwise stance for all the route notes. It is normally a simple matter to reverse each section by reference to a map and by intelligent observation at path junctions and the like. With this book in your hand you are extremely unlikely to go astray!

Route notes are accurate when going to press and will take the guesswork out of tricky stretches of path while sketching in points of interest along the way. To assist forward planning of both day walks and continuous long-distance hikes, the coast path has been divided into 21 sections, a day's walk in length and beginning and ending at places where there are amenities for refreshment or accommodation (or access inland to them). Three longer stages of roughly a week each are introduced by brief descriptions. These are suggestions only and may well be exceeded by strong walkers, or split into shorter increments if desired. For distances between places along the way, consult the mileage table at the back of this book.

Each section begins with a summary of its length, the kind of terrain and gradients to be expected, along with details of amenities and access points. An attempt has been made to grade the walking for difficulty, though such an exercise will always be subjective. 'Easy' means mostly flat going on good paths, tracks or urban pavements. 'Moderate' means average gradients of the kind encountered in gentle hill country, with well-defined paths of good surface. 'More difficult' denotes rough, awkward terrain or considerable ups and downs, unsuitable for very young, elderly or inexperienced walkers. 'Strenuous' means successive big ascents and descents on rugged paths, often steep and remote from roads or habitations.

In the text, places reached on the path are followed in brackets by the amenities they provide. 'All shops, services and accommodation' suggests the availability of most consumer goods, a range of places to eat and stay at, and the existence of banks, Post Office, telephones, toilets etc. A few other features such as Information Centres, museums, etc. are also mentioned but the lists cannot claim to be comprehensive in scope.

Alternative routings (variants) appear in smaller type, while notable places or features along the path are picked out in heavier type for quick identification.

Sketch maps accompanying the text are not intended to supplant the use of Ordnance Survey maps and will not help you re-establish your position if you become completely lost in a sea mist or low cloud and driving rain, or if you have strayed badly off route. However, used in conjunction with the detailed Route Notes, the sketch maps will steer you happily down the coast - for 99% of the time problem-free. Drawn to scale, they paint a broad picture of the walking ahead and what to look out for, enabling you to identify linear progress quickly and easily. (Please note that twists and turns round coastal indentations cannot be readily accommodated in the page layout, so always refer to direction north on each map to orientate it with compass or OS sheet.) With this book open in front of you, the sketch maps read from the bottom of the page to the top, corresponding with the coast unfolding ahead.

No individual or organisation can hope to monitor all changes which take place on the path through erosion, land-use alteration or obstructions. It would therefore be appreciated if walkers would note down any significant new cliff-falls or unofficial path diversions etc. on the blank pages provided at the end of this book. The South West Way Association would like to hear from you - please write giving details of your observations to Eric Wallis, 'Windlestraw', Penquit, Ermington, Nr. IVYBRIDGE, Devon PL21 0LU.

The book concludes with a list of Useful Addresses, a Bibliography, a Coast Path Code, a Sea-bathing Code and a Distances Table.

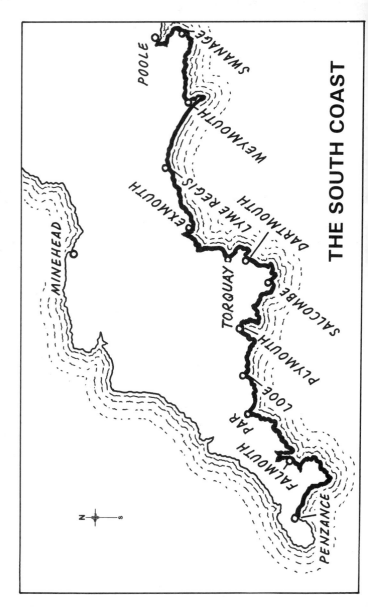

THE SOUTH COAST

POOLE

SWANAGE

WEYMOUTH

DARTMOUTH

LYME REGIS

EXMOUTH

TORQUAY

SALCOMBE

PLYMOUTH

LOOE

PAR

FALMOUTH

PENZANCE

MINEHEAD

N
S

Approaching Mullion Cove

SOUTH WEST WAY

Book 2
THE SOUTH COAST

CHAPTER 1
Penzance to Plymouth
(124 miles - 200km)

Flat walking east from Penzance leads past the evocative island castle of St. Michael's Mount and the smuggling haunt of Prussia Cove to a long beach at Praa Sands. Mining ruins and rugged gradients follow as the path reaches Porthleven harbour and skirts the freshwater Loe Pool on a shingle ridge. The much photographed Mullion Cove heralds a change to serpentine rock and marvellously open clifftop to Kynance Cove and the Lizard lighthouse, Britain's most southerly mainland point.

Undulating above a rocky shoreline, you pass a lifeboat station and the pretty fishing village of Cadgwith before engaging a tougher section round Black Head to Coverack. Wooded low cliffs to Lowland Point precede diversions through a stone quarry and on country lanes via Porthoustock to Porthallow. Soon you veer inland, wade a creek, round a headland and take the river ferry from picturesque Helford. Estuary shore inlets and promontories lead out round Rosemullion Head to the beaches and port of Falmouth.

Several options exist to reach the Roseland Peninsula across Carrick Roads where the coast path resumes on unspoiled cliffs past Portscatho and over Nare Head. Tiny Portloe and popular little bays give way to the Dodman, a major headland beyond which huddles Gorran Haven. Not far ahead lies the lively fishing harbour of Mevagissey and a varied walk, becoming increasingly built-up, to the china-clay port of Par.

Soon back in magnificent scenery, Fowey's sheltered anchorage sees the start of remote and strenuous clifftop walking to much visited Polperro and the river mouth harbour town of Looe. Woodland then the beach itself at Seaton are soon followed by a detour round Tregantle Fort military training camp and the sands or cliff road towards Rame Head. Beyond this headland, pleasant walking above Plymouth Sound takes you through twin fishing villages and a country park to the Cremyll ferry and Plymouth city.

SECTION 1 - Penzance to Porthleven;   13 miles (21km)
Flat walking past the Scilly Isles heliport leads to Marazion and a chance

to visit famous St. Michael's Mount. The path, subject to bad erosion and with a couple of short beach stretches, then skirts low cliffs round the edges of cultivated fields before improving dramatically at Cudden Point. The erstwhile smuggling haunt of Prussia Cove and some fine clifftop walking bring you to the popular beach resort of Praa Sands. Evocative copper mining ruins are passed close by the path and gradients become rather tougher until you arrive at the harbour town of Porthleven. Grading - easy then moderate.

Shops, services and accommodation at Marazion (also causeway and ferry to St. Michael's Mount). Pub, shop off-route at Perranuthnoe. Shop, pub, refreshments and accommodation at Praa Sands.

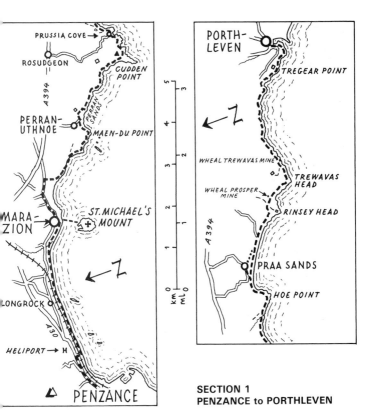

SECTION 1
PENZANCE to PORTHLEVEN

37

In conjunction with Newlyn just to the west, Penzance possesses all the facilities likely to be needed by coastal walkers. It is well used to receiving visitors, being British Rail's south-western main line terminus, a popular holiday base for exploring the Land's End and Lizard peninsulas and the setting-off point by ferry or helicopter to the Isles of Scilly. Accommodation and local public transport are both plentiful and there is a youth hostel a mile north-west of the town centre at Castle Horneck.

Put on the map by the opening of its Great Western Railway station in the 1850's, Penzance benefitted from better communications with the rest of Britain, particularly in relation to tourism and the transportation of Cornwall's early vegetables and flowers. To reach this far-flung corner of Britain is, nevertheless, still a somewhat daunting journey for most of us, despite improving roads and inter-city trains: beyond Plymouth the pace of travel is slowed by river estuaries, villages and a hilly countryside. To get the most out of visiting Penzance, see the Tourist Information Office opposite St. John's Hall in the main shopping thoroughfare - Alverton Street.

Leaving Penzance first by the A30 then the coastal Longrock road, look out for the coast path turn-off, crossing a railway sidings footbridge just before the heliport. This is a busy, noisy stretch of walking, close to road, railway and possibly fumey helicopters, but looking towards St. Michael's Mount from the path along the back of the beach is some compensation. (You could catch a bus to Marazion.)

Once past Longrock's industrial estate *(pub and shops in Longrock village)* and some converted railway carriages, you come to a car park *(cafe; toilets)* on the coast road. From here, either go down steps in the sea wall and walk along the beach or continue along the pavement. Road and footbridge over the river draining Marazion Marsh are adjacent, whereafter you head across grassy car parking *(cafes; toilets)*, over the slipway and keep forward (past Beach Cafe to the right) along a lane meeting the main street in **MARAZION** *(shops and services – limited bank opening; accommodation; cafes, restaurants and pubs; Post Office, telephone; buses for Penzance; aquarium; causeway and ferry for St. Michael's Mount).*

NOTES ON ST. MICHAEL'S MOUNT: A place of Celtic legend and Christian pilgrimage, the island is crowned by a spectacular 14th century castle and the tower of its 12th century church. Edward the Confessor built the original Benedictine Priory in 1044 as a dependence of Mont St. Michel's abbey in Brittany. With its community around the base and a connecting causeway, St. Michael's Mount does resemble its Brittany counterpart; much smaller and

Marazion, from St.Michael's Mount

unexploited however, and visiting it is considerably more pleasant. The St. Aubyn family, whose seat the Mount has been since 1659, donated the property to the National Trust in 1954 and the present Lord St. Aubyn still resides there. The National Trust has a shop and 2 cafes on the island and operates an audio-visual introductory show. Access is by foot over the causeway at low tide, or by ferry during high tide in the summer months - confirm tide times at the slipway. Grounds and buildings are open weekdays except Thursday during April and May; Thursdays included from 1st June to 31st October.

The onward coast path routing now continues up Marazion's busy main street to the top of the hill and on along the level until 200m past Mount Haven Hotel, where a sign clearly points right through a gate opposite a minor road junction. Walk down the track and keep ahead at the bottom between field fence and hedge to a bouldery and pebbly beach. The low earth cliffs are manifestly subject to serious erosion and the path has long since slipped away: possible future re-routings on this section. Walk along over rocks and watch for a waymark post directing you back up left to regain the path at an acorn stile.

Continuing at the perimeter of crop fields, there are unexpectedly goods views back to St. Michael's Mount and Marazion before once again a beach detour is necessary. At the author's last visit, this was a thoroughly objectionable 300m over washed-up debris and awkward large pebbles coated with slimy, smelly and fly-infested seaweed! Beyond a stream, the path returns to a higher level outside private land, then more fields. The walking is perilously near the edge in places and it cannot be long before re-routing becomes imperative.

A succession of minor pebbly coves leads round Maen-du Point where you veer inland behind houses towards Perran Sands. *(Just up the road left is the village of* **PERRANUTHNOE** *- pub; Post Office/ Store; toilets; telephone; car park).* Cross the road and walk up a lane almost opposite for 400m. Fork right on a track past a house for 100m then turn right again. A further right turn near a bungalow takes you down a path to the sea's edge. This detour is due, of course, to cliff subsidence.

More crop fields are skirted, this time inside their seaward boundary, then you are out over rough pasture above Trevean Cove, keeping landward of a wall. With surroundings improving by the minute, this is coastal walking of high quality - a dipping and rising path through gorse and wild flowers with superb cliff and ocean views.

There is access out along the jagged crest of Cudden Point, scene of numerous shipwrecks, but the coast path climbs over its shoulder to another surprise revelation. Closer now than from Carn-du near Lamorna, recognisable landmarks such as Loe Bar lead the eye round to Lizard Point. Stay round the seaward cliff edge and onto a stony track by a thatched cottage and postbox above **PRUSSIA COVE** *(small car park).* Down to the right stands a post associated with the salvage of HMS Warspite in April 1947. The ageing 30,000 ton battleship had been en route for the breakers yard after seeing service in two World Wars when she was blown onto rocks here, her crew heroically rescued by the Penlee lifeboat.

Prussia Cove takes its name from the former 'King of Prussia' inn, kept by the colourful 18th century Carter family, whose smuggling exploits in defiance of Customs men is writ large in local folklore.

Go up the track and turn right at the junction (left leads from the car park). You continue down round Bessy's Cove, a one-time landing place for smuggled brandy and named after Bessy Burrow who ran a nearby alehouse. Today it is an idyllic little suntrap flanked by rock pools and much visited in summer. The BBC filmed here for their 'Poldark' series.

Swinging left through an intriguing circular space between façades of Porth-en-Alls house (holiday flats), stay on the track and fork right

Praa Sands

past a row of 19th century Coastguard cottages to an acorn gate by a small quarry. At the path fork ahead, keep right along between bushes of gorse and thorn above Kenneggy Sands (these can be reached by the sure-footed down a path ending in a ladder and rope!). Duck-boarding crosses a spectacular reed bed, then you drop to cross a stream at Pestreath Cove before climbing on round Hoe Point.

Soon the buildings of **PRAA (or PRAH) SANDS** appear *(accommodation; camping; pub; beach cafe; telephone; toilets. Up road inland -supermarket; caravan park; Post Office).* A short downhill walk brings you to this rather sprawling settlement with its mile of golden sands. You immediately pass a cafe, fish and chip bar, toilets and telephone, turning right on the back road to a large car park. More pleasant then is to continue over the golf links by the wire fence, eventually turning inland on a slatted walkway to join the back road lined with salubrious properties behind the dunes. (If the tide is low, it is possible to simply walk along Praa Sands.)

Concurrent with the end of the private road and the beach, turn down right through a rough car park and climb onto Lesceave Cliff ahead - donated to the National Trust by the family of William Treloar who had great affection for the area. Ignore the right fork out to Rinsey Head, passing instead an old railway carriage chalet, crossing the Rinsey Head house access track and a National Trust car park for **WHEAL PROSPER MINE.**

Wheal Prosper's short life producing copper ended in 1860. The

National Trust has spent some £4,000 restoring the engine house and chimney to a safe condition and though somewhat 'manicured' in appearance for the author's taste, the buildings were undoubtedly saved from collapse, to be enjoyed henceforth for their historical interest. Signs of mining hereabouts are attributable to a temporary geological change from slates to granite and its associated ore deposits.

Lovely clifftop walking through gorse follows. Cross a big wall stile into the seaward field and another stile by a gate, then proceed along a farm track on Trewavas Head. A wire fence and more gorse lead round above the impressive ruins of **WHEAL TREWAVAS MINE** whose copper-ore production was brought to an untimely end around 1850 when the sea broke in, reputedly during the annual underground dinner! It is worth making a small detour to the cliff edge for a close-up inspection of the chimney and engine house, and to look back at the other buildings.

You now drop and climb over the stream valley at Trequean, facing banded rock strata. In the next dip at Tremearne are steps to a shingly beach and a sign indicating progress - Rinsey 1½, Praa Sands 2½ miles. Soon the path is held tightly between stout fencing round the first of several deep indentations. A big landslip in March 1988 necessitated a new path line being established - just how serious the slippage was can be ascertained by noting a 20m gap in a banked wall. The cliff edge is crumbling badly all along here, so the advice is to keep well back.

Beyond Tregear Point *(hotel near path)*, you will pass a cross on a white plinth erected in March 1949 in memory of mariners drowned on this coast. In case they were heathen, shipwreck victims were interred in mass graves near where they washed ashore - until the Rev. Gryll's act of 1808 which allowed bodies to be properly buried in consecrated ground.

About 100m past the cross, look down right to see a large, polished boulder of brown gneiss weighing 20 tons. Known as Giant's Rock, it is an 'erratic', probably deposited by an iceberg during the last Ice Age.

Our way soon joins a very wide path, passes a telephone box and forks right to the harbour town of **PORTHLEVEN** *(all shops, services and accommodation, campsite; cafes, restaurants and pubs; Post Office; buses for Falmouth, Penzance and Helston; car parks; toilets; early closing Wednesday)*.

The granite mole and quays were constructed at the beginning of the last century, the inner breakwater being added around 1855. At that time Porthleven was a thriving fishing port, handling general

Porthleven Harbour

cargoes too until the railway came to Cornwall. Although it has dwindled to a shadow of its former self, the fishing trade here is still alive, lending an authentic working atmosphere to the harbour. Tourism is also important and visitors often link Porthleven with the market town of Helston, 3 miles (5km) inland.

SECTION 2 - Porthleven to the Lizard; 13 miles (21km)

After walking Loe Bar shingle bank, the cliff edge path undulates above coves notorious for shipwreck and reaches a seashore church in a dramatic setting. Popular Poldhu Cove and the Marconi Monument lead on to Mullion Cove, an archetypal Cornish fishing harbour. Serpentine rock now dominates the rugged landscape and views take in all Mount's Bay as the path continues over beautiful grassy clifftop not far from a Royal Navy Helicopter School. A moorland stretch, a steep drop over a stream valley and the way is clear along to Kynance Cove with its extraordinary rock islands. Further small streams are crossed before you arrive at Britain's southernmost mainland point - the Lizard. Grading - mostly moderate but more difficult in places. Very exposed in bad weather.

Pub just inland from Gunwalloe Fishing Cove. Nearby accommodation at Polurrian Cove. Seasonal refreshments, camping, car parks at Mullion Cove. Shops, services and accommodation, pub, buses at Mullion, a mile

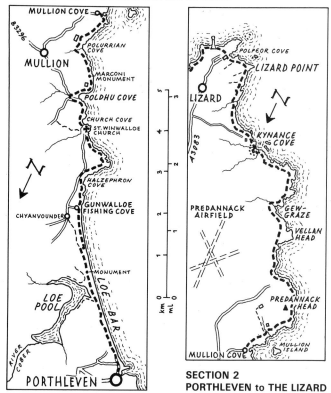

SECTION 2
PORTHLEVEN to THE LIZARD

inland. Seasonal refreshment, car parks at Kynance Cove.

Walk round past the 200 year old Ship Inn, once a haunt of smugglers, and skirt Porthleven's harbour basin right round to the clock tower on the Bickford-Smith Institute. Cliff Road leads on south-east past a Coastguard lookout above Porthleven Sands. Foundations of the one-time coast road are subject to wave damage and only walkers could use it at the author's last visit. On both sides are signs of more mining activity, this time the Wheal Penrose lead mine which closed in 1844 but is thought to have been worked in Roman times.

At the entrance to the National Trust's Penrose Estate, fork right down onto **LOE BAR** *(emergency telephone)*. This extraordinary natural dam of chalk flint shingle holds back Helston's River Cober to form Loe Pool, a freshwater lake surrounded by luxuriant vegetation and an unusual variety of tree species. Designated a Site of Special Scientific Interest, Loe Pool is famous for its bird population. If you've time, there is a pleasant pathway round the lake, open during daylight hours - allow at least 2 hours for the full circuit.

After heavy rainfall, Helston is subject to flooding by the blocked River Cober. At such times a drainage channel is cut through Loe Bar - the last time in 1984 by Water Authority bulldozers.

After a shingle trudge, a pathside memorial cross is passed, dedicated to Henry Trengrouse. Son of a Helston cabinet maker, he spent a lifetime developing the rocket-fired lifeline after witnessing the tragic loss of HMS Anson in December 1807 on Loe Bar, when 120 lives were lost.

Grassy slopes run ahead to the clifftop path but a safer alternative veers diagonally left to follow a wall and enters a lane between fields. Turn right at an old quarry back to the cliff edge path which leads down to **GUNWALLOE FISHING COVE** *(pub, Post Office, telephone - just inland in Chyanvounder hamlet)*. Clear waymarking is part of the local authority's work in maintaining a safe path despite incessant erosion. You leave the cove behind a bungalow, climbing steeply to around 200ft. (60m) and joining the road briefly above Halzephron Cove. Follow signs round a field edge and rejoin the original coast path at a stile. You touch Winnianton Farm's lane, with Goonhilly Earth Station now only 4 miles (6.5km) away to the east, and detour right, onto Jangye-ryn cliffs above Dollar Cove before dropping to a small car park *(summer refreshment hut; toilets)*.

This area was the scene of 2 early shipwrecks. The Portuguese 'St. Anthony' was driven ashore in 1526 at Gunwalloe laden with bullion, silver and plate valued at £16,000. In the 1780's an unnamed Spanish ship struck rocks near Church Cove and spilled many tons of gold and silver coins into a gully. Over the years, repeated salvage operations have been mounted to retrieve this accumulation of treasure trove. Techniques included damming the gully and pumping it dry, tunnelling beneath it to release embedded coins (the miners almost drowned!), pumping and sieving sand by the ton. Only a fraction of the treasure was found and this may be due to periodic substantial movements of the sandy sea bed in Mount's Bay. Even today, finding a single coin by chance is still possible.

A wall on the right leads you to **ST. WINWALLOE CHURCH,** its back to the sea and prevailing weather behind a protective rock among the sandhills on the edge of Church Cove. It is not a secure site and

Poldhu Cove

may be vulnerable to eventual inundation by storm waves on this beleaguered coast. Founded by Brittany monks in the 6th century and dedicated to St. Winwalloe, a contemporary Breton Abbot, the present building dates from the 14th or 15th century, its bell tower possibly earlier. Sunday afternoon services are held during the summer.

With Mullion Golf Course over to your left, follow the wide track fairly steeply uphill to a car park on Carrag-a-pilez cliff and drop down the road to **POLDHU COVE** *(beach cafe; car park; toilets; buses for Helston and Lizard)*. Poldhu is Cornish for black pool; the cove has a large expanse of sand at low tide, is open to Atlantic surf and becomes quite crowded in peak season.

Cross the road bridge and turn right up a private drive towards the large building ahead - formerly an hotel, now a residential home. Near the top turn down right and walk round to **MARCONI'S MONUMENT**. Erected in 1937 after the transmitting station masts had been dismantled, the granite pillar commemorates Guglielmo Marconi's momentous invention of the wireless from which all modern telecommunications derive. In an age of satellites and fibre-optics, it is pertinent to recall that until Marconi's first transatlantic radio message of December 12th 1901, it was not known whether radio waves would follow the earth's curvature and make long-distance exchanges a reality. Interestingly, the first transatlantic television pictures were received at nearby Goonhilly Earth Station in

July 1962.

There are fine views back along the coast and forward to the long, flat shape of Mullion Island. Just before Polurrian Cove *(nearby accommodation; toilets)*, fork right and drop back to the little footbridge. The stepped climb out is more strenuous - an alternative, longer zig-zag eases the gradient. Now on a stony track, walk up beneath the footbridge to the start of a bungalow estate. Turn right along the access track for clifftop properties *(B&B)* and fork right to arrive at a road turning circle by the imposing Mullion Cove Hotel. From the little car park's seaward end, a path descends steps with views below over **MULLION COVE** which is soon reached *(small seasonal cafe; up lane are toilets, gift shop, camping and car parks. Over a mile further is*

The Marconi Monument

MULLION *village - shops and services; accommodation; pub; buses; interesting 15th century church; early closing Wednesday).*

Perhaps the definitive Cornish fishing harbour, Mullion Cove appears in publicity photographs, guidebooks and no doubt holiday albums everwhere. In fact, Porth Mellin - its real name - is small-scale and before the breakwater was built in 1895, fishing boats ran the gauntlet of swell and wind to enter the cliff-bound inlet. The place is best seen off-season, but loses much of its appeal in grey, dismal weather.

The coast path leaves a short distance inland round the back of houses, climbing onto Mullion Cliff and past a National Nature Reserve sign for The Lizard. The Lizard Peninsula is of special geological and botanical interest, with many rare grasses, plants and flowers in evidence. Serpentine becomes the dominant rock type - it is uncommon and named after its resemblance to snake's skin, so the area is well known. Local craftspeople carve and polish the greenish stone into ornaments, for sale in workshops and stalls.

In good visibility, the sweep of Mount's Bay right back to Tater-du lighthouse is breathtaking in scope. Levelling off over gorsey heath, the way allows time and breath to gaze down at lichen-tinged cliffs and Mullion Island, streaked with guano from countless seabirds nesting there.

A stile points the way ahead over a little stream valley near a white house, whereafter you pass through a handgate and continue outside a field fence round Predannack Head. This is easy walking on delightful grassy clifftop, punctuated perhaps by the busy clatter of helicopters from Predannack Airfield. As part of R.N.A.S. Culdrose, the airfield supports a Royal Naval Helicopter School and is associated with Dr. Barnes Wallis of 'Dambuster' fame. The helicopter base and naval air station is the largest in Europe and is responsible for air-sea rescue, so the buzz of activity - practice as well as real emergencies - is hardly surprising.

At a bench by a rocky viewpoint, the coast path angles back down over another stream above Ogo-dour Cove which can be muddy from cattle. A few stiles are all that interrupt a further stretch of gentle walking, but beware the collapsing cliff edge in places. Gradually, surroundings begin to resemble a bleak and boggy Pennine moor, especially if you are head down against wind and rain! Parallel tracks eventually converge and The Lizard buildings become visible on the flat heathland horizon. From an acorn post, the coast path rounds a cliff indentation where a small waymark (easy to miss) points off left to cut across Vellan Head.

Kynance Cove

An unstable and potentially dangerous stile is followed by an unexpectedly steep and rugged drop to Gew-graze (or Soapy Cove)., An old soapstone quarry here once sent its 'steatite' for use in Wedgwood and Worcester porcelain *(possible wild camping pitch)*.

From the climb out, look back at the beetling cliffs and perhaps detour slightly to seaward for a glance down Pigeon Ogo ('ogo' means cave) with its nesting seabird colonies. There is no clear path over the dense turf, but keep uphill and aim for the cliff edge again above Rill Cove (where it is said the Spanish Armada was first sighted in 1588). The path now evident again, walking is without effort unless the weather is inclement, when the going can be very hard against a head wind. Small rocky outcrops and several trods lead on towards the rock islands of Kynance Cove. Before long you drop right from one finger post to another lower down and at a metal post turn right down the steps to the footbridge at **KYNANCE COVE** *(beach cafe; car parks and toilets on the clifftop)*.

An outstanding beauty spot, Kynance Cove's popularity dates back to the mid-19th century when it became a haunt of excursionists, artists and writers, including Alfred Lord Tennyson, Prince Albert and the Royal children. Though only 300m across, the cove's real fascination lies in the dramatic islands of serpentine rock which at low tide rear from an expanse of golden sand. The largest is called Asparagus Rock, others have names such as the Sugarloaf, Steeple

Rock and The Bishop. Around the islands' bases and to the west of the cove are several exciting and interconnected caves - The Ladies Bathing Pool, The Drawing Room, etc., as well as some sensational blowholes.

Provided the tide is low enough, cross the back of the stoney cove and climb a well used path on the right to the clifftop. If, however, waves and high water prevent this, walk up between the beach cafe and a cottage to find steps up the valley side, leading onto a path through gorse and meeting a broad track. Continue ahead (right) off the hairpin bend to reach another track and proceed up a stepped and popular path to the clifftop car park *(seasonal refreshments; toilets).* Already a car park in the 1930's, the National Trust acquired this plot of land in 1986. They demolished the old house and shop, laying new emphasis on the conservation of natural beauty and local ecology.

Walk forward outside the car park wall as the path undulates pleasantly along, re-routed in places to avoid the Holestrow landslip area. You drop to cross a couple of streams near signs of small-scale serpentine quarrying here and there, before a training post and stone stile behind a jutting prow of rock announce your rounding of **LIZARD POINT**. The distinction of being Britain's most southerly point belongs marginally to ground above Polpeor Cove and this is reached by passing the now disused Coastguard lookout and crossing another stream valley. *(Path left direct to* **LIZARD** *village - 1 mile: shops, accommodation; pub; cafe; Post Office; buses; early closing Wednesday.)* A final short climb and you arrive at the southernmost mainland point with its 2 seasonal cafes and serpentine shops. *(Car park and toilets up lane left, which also leads to Lizard village but is busy with cars in summer.)* The coast path crosses the little stony car park and passes round the cliff edge below Lizard lighthouse and foghorn.

Rarely is a lighthouse more needed than this one. Because the Lizard headland protrudes into shipping lanes through the English Channel, more wrecks have occurred here than anywhere else on the south coast. The very first fire beacon was erected on June 29th 1619 by Sir John Killigrew, Falmouth's founding father, but this example of private enterprise (a levy was to be 'extracted' from passing ships!) was so fiercely opposed by locals and the Trinity Brethren of London that the beacon was not operational for another 20 years. A continuous light has existed, however, since 1640, first fired by wood and coal. Oil lamps were introduced in 1812 and replaced by electric arc lights in 1878. The present 4 million candle-power lighthouse, its building dating from 1757, is open to public visits on weekday afternoons.

Rounding Lizard Point

SECTION 3 - Lizard to Porthallow (or St. Keverne);   14 miles (23km)

Lighthouse, Coastguard station and Lifeboat station are passed in quick succession as the path turns north-east and becomes more sheltered in character. Above precipitous cliffs it drops to Cadgwith, another attractive Cornish fishing village, before more undulating clifftop and a drop through the pretty Poltesco valley bring you to the small beach resort of Kennack Sands. Beyond, the way is less well walked and the going is rougher underfoot. Rounding Black Head is a minor milestone and the harder gradients are left behind for a scenic approach to Coverack. In and out of trees almost at sea level, you reach Lowlands Point and negotiate Dean Quarry before turning inland with options to make for the amenities of St. Keverne or to continue on the official route to Porthoustock and country lanes to Porthallow.   Grading - moderate but more difficult between Kennack Sands and Coverack.

Refreshments and accommodation at Cadgwith. Seasonal refreshments at Kennack Sands. Shops, accommodation and refreshments at Coverack. Limited accommodation and refreshments at Porthoustock.

Beyond the Lizard lighthouse, a short detour right will reveal a collapsed sea cave formed in February 1847 and known as the Lion's Den: proceed with care! Steps lead steeply down to the rocky inlet of Housel Cove, after which walkers are invited for drinks, snacks and meals by Housel Bay Hotel's signboard. The wooden shack above Polledan cleft was used by Marconi in early radio experiments.

At a gate ahead *(track left back to Lizard village - 750m)*, the coast

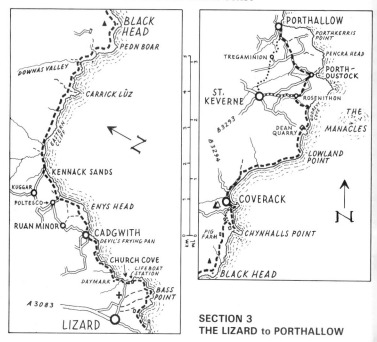

SECTION 3
THE LIZARD to PORTHALLOW

path swings ½-right to pass seaward of the conspicuous, white castellated Bass Point House - until 1969 a Lloyd's signal station. Close to the path is a manned Coastguard lookout and a red-white navigation marker.

Turning north, you very soon reach the modern Lizard-Cadgwith Lifeboat station in Kilcobben Cove, replacing those at Lizard and Cadgwith in 1961. Descend a few steps by the boathouse and continue round to **CHURCH COVE,** coming up inland 20m to turn right through a gate and along the track towards a day mark on the hill ahead. (5 minutes up the road from Church Cove past picturesque thatched cottages - surprisingly holiday lets - stands Landewednack church surrounded by elms. A further 10 minutes to Lizard village.)

Climbing now through old serpentine workings to the clifftop path, you pass the big, diamond-shaped day mark and drop over a stream valley. The narrowing way is pinched between fields near Gwavas Farm and the precipitous cliffs along to another collapsed sea cave

The Lizard/Cadgwith Lifeboat House, Kilcobben Cove

-Devil's Cauldron - and a small copse of dwarf elms on the right. You descend attractively through private gardens and past cottages to the road and **CADGWITH** *(accommodation; cafe/restaurant; inn; telephone; car park 400m up inland; shops at Ruan Minor 800m inland).*

Like so many Cornish fishing villages, Cadgwith once enjoyed modest prosperity from pilchards which were netted in huge numbers before the shoals dwindled and finally disappeared towards the turn of the last century. A lifeboat was stationed here from 1867 until the new Lizard/Cadgwith boat was installed.

Our way proceeds along this charming little waterfront with its fishing boats and groups of blue-jerseyed fishermen - not to mention the many summer sightseers - and turns right just past the inn at the start of the road hill. At first climbing, then following field edges onto gorsey clifftop, the coast path provides a delightful meander round Enys Head; note the novel gate/stile design!

Keeping generally to seaward, you reach a gate which leads on down to the Poltesco valley. Watch out for a right turn by the National Trust sign and cross the unusually airy footbridge in the wooded ravine. Until 1889, a workshop - the Lizard Serpentine Company -manufactured large items such as shop facades, mantlepieces and tables from serpentine rock just below on the beach at Carleon Cove; the buildings are being restored by the National Trust.

A longish climb out the other side now ensues. Ignore a track off left and stay outside the field wall. Farther on, the right path fork is easier and less rocky but gains the same height as the left fork and they converge at the top to level off along the seaward perimeter of Sea Acres Caravan Site. Follow acorn waymarks down to the narrow country lane (don't try short-cutting right through brambles!) which brings you out at **KENNACK SANDS** *(summer cafe; beach shop; car park; toilets).*

From now until Black Head is rounded, the way is noticeably less well walked. There are some stiff gradients to contend with and the going becomes rocky and tortuous at times so allow plenty of time and energy for the 5 miles (8km) to Coverack.

Walk along the back of Kennack Sands, renowned for its varied pebbles of pink granite, gabbro and green and red serpentine, and follow the lane over the neck of Caerverracks headland. The path leaves the sea wall at the far end of this little beach and climbs fairly relentlessly up the rough shoulder of Eastern Cliff (be careful not to go inland here). Through bracken and heather, the narrow trod continues along clifftops then drops to cross a stream (rather awkwardly) below Poldowrian Farm. Above Spernic Cove a little farther on, be sure not to follow a field track ½-right which leads out to Carrick Lûz (Great Grey Rock) headland. Keep ahead here along by a wall on the left and cross over the farm track to Borgwitha. Watch for a small stone waymark where the onward path leaves the farm track over rough ground behind Lankidden Cove.

A conspicuous stile brings you into a field whose cliff edge fence (right) is followed steeply downhill. Further stiles were of very poor construction at the author's last visit and will do nothing to ease your descent into Downas valley. Cross the stream footbridge, ignoring a path off left, and attack the substantial climb out on the seaward path to a stout National Trust stile at the top.

With a wall on your left, the cliff path rounds Beagle Point, crosses Beagle Hole, a marshy depression, and goes through a wall at the top beyond. Now on a plain clifftop track, you pass a small memorial cross, go over a stile and round behind Pedn Boar headland. The nearby paint testing panels belong to British Insulated Callenders Cables Co.

Still outside field walls and a stream valley later, you reach the Coastguard lookout on **BLACK HEAD,** a minor turning point on the coast. In a few metres there is a wall stile and in another 25m it is necessary to keep right, leaving the field on your left. The sinuous path (periodically cleared of undergrowth) continues over heather, bracken and gorse, with Coverack's Headland Hotel prominent ahead.

After a tricky little stream crossing and more weaving in and out, the way swings inland towards Trewillis pig farm. Keep to the seaward path outside a wire fence and proceed ahead between hedges. As you pass the piggery, the air may not seem as fresh as it has been! Beyond a large tank you are out on open waste ground; cross a rutted farm track and enter a copse which is preceded by a large granite stile. Over the brook, walk up through the trees and bear right past caravans to a bungalow and tarmac lane.

There are 2 options for entering Coverack. The most direct but non-coastal route turns left and in about 150m turns right through a stile and descends fields. At the bottom, a line of dazzlingly white fishermen's cottages lead on down to a Wesleyan chapel at a road junction. Here turn off right above a small playground and go down steps, turning left past a black house to emerge at the 'charity' car park by the Paris Hotel.

The true coastal footpath with superior views turns right from the bungalow towards Headland Hotel, but just before reaching it veers left (waymarked) and drops on a newish path. From the junction at the bottom, paths go out onto Chynhalls Point with its Iron Age promontory fort and superb views, and to Porthbeer Cove round to the right. However, the coast path turns left above a sheltered, bouldery foreshore flanked by luxuriant vegetation, to reach the lane of fishermen's cottages and the route as described above.

The Paris Hotel is named after the 10,000 ton American liner which was stranded on nearby Lowland Point in 1899. Its large complement of 750 passengers were taken off unharmed by the Falmouth and Porthoustock lifeboats and 6 weeks later the great ship was success-fully refloated.

Turning left at the hotel brings you along into **COVERACK** (*drinks; meals; accommodation; campsite; youth hostel; Post Office/General Store; telephone; buses; car parks; toilets*). With a tiny harbour just capable of sheltering its few fishing boats, Coverack maintained a seine net for pilchard fishing long after the industry had all but ended in the rest of Cornwall; the old cellars can still be seen on the harbour. Today the village plays host mostly to pleasure craft and scuba divers - even the Lifeboat station has become a restaurant! Nevertheless, the main street makes for a pleasant dawdle, with views north-east to Lowland Point.

Above the shingle beach round beyond the harbour, the road swings up left near a bus shelter. Turn right here and walk along the shady lane servicing shoreline properties. After about 1km the surface becomes stony and you follow this track up past a gate, watching for an acorn post and path down right (straight on leads to St. Keverne).

The coast path has been laboriously filled in with small rocks and stone chippings, greatly reducing its original marshiness; it undulates agreeably along in and out of trees not far above the sea. A stream and stile lead onwards and there are good views back to Coverack; at low tide the bouldery beach is surprisingly extensive. Cattle hooves and several brooks conspire to add to the general wetness on this flat stretch. Geologically speaking, it is a raised beach and just inland can be made out a 200ft. (60m) line of cliffs which formed the original shore. It is thought that the land here rose up when released from a vast pressure of ice at the end of the last Ice Age 10,000 years ago.

At **LOWLANDS POINT** (National Trust), you are almost at sea level and will be confronted by a graphic reminder of how plastic jetsam from busy shipping lanes causes a build-up of unsightly litter. Miscellaneous rubbish is strewn over the beach and has been blown and washed across the immediate hinterland.

Having passed a metal post and curious circular mound, Dean Quarry is sighted ahead. A pathside notice-board announces that

Dean Quarry

blasting occurs between 10-10.30am. 1-1.30pm. and 5-6.30pm., with warnings given by red flag and continuous hooter. If you are unlucky enough to arrive at the wrong moment, it is advisable to wait and if necessary shelter in the little rusty cabin provided!

Now the coast path is forced to negotiate the quarry complex, but to give credit where it is due, clear waymarking has been installed. First you climb past extensive terraced workings (the quarry produces road-stone) and up an old spoil heap. At one time the route swung left inland and you can still walk that way to Porthoustock via Rosenithon. The true coastal path, however, veers seaward, well signed and indicated where necessary by yellow railings as you thread through the works installations (beware quarry vehicles). Stay seaward down a quarry roadway past mountains of grey gravel and follow it briefly uphill round Dean Point, then swinging right down to **GODREVY COVE.**

During this industrial interlude, take a good look out to sea, for a mile (1,500m) offshore lies the notorious Manacles, a reef with a name as sinister as its reputation. It is estimated that nearly 1,000 people have lost their lives in shipwrecks on this 1½ square miles of rocks, almost submerged at high tide and spread across the southern approaches to Falmouth. Although marked by a large red buoy on its seaward edge, most ships give the Manacles a wide berth. One disaster concerned the 7,000 ton passenger ship 'Mohegan' which struck at 7.00pm. on October 14th 1898; among 106 drowned were all her officers and most of the passengers. Even more catastrophic was the emigrant ship 'John' in which 200 died in 1855.

The onward route at Godrevy Cove used to be easily missed, but recent waymark posts should clarify it for some time to come unless obscured by reeds. Walk along the sandy/shingly beach and after crossing the stream mouth, follow it inland, angling right a little. Veer back to the stream and cross it on a plank bridge, whereafter a metal handgate leads you into a field. Go straight up the edge, over a stone stile and through the farmyard. Keep straight on up the lane past a thatched cottage in Rosenithon hamlet and turn right up the country road. (Less than a mile away to the left lies St. Keverne with shops, 2 pubs and accommodation. A good footpath can then be taken direct to Porthallow via Tregaminion.)

At a right bend, look for a finger post pointing the way off left across fields, linking gaps in old banked hedges towards a house ahead. Opposite the house is a gate/stile back onto the road which this field-walking has short-cut. Turn down left, right at the junction and on down to **PORTHOUSTOCK** *(B&B; cafe; telephone; car park; toilets)*.

A busy port handling cargoes of stone from nearby quarries and with its own lifeboat until 1942, Porthoustock is now a pleasant, if unremarkable, little bay used by the boating fraternity and scuba divers.

The official coast path diverts inland again, this time to bypass the disused quarries around Pencra Head and Porthkerris Point. Those with local knowledge and a disregard for the rights of way issue might well walk through the old quarry workings, but bona fide walkers should not be tempted!

Instead, leave Porthoustock uphill on the country road north-west towards Porthallow and fork left on a path which short-cuts about 500m of road walking. Continue through Trenance hamlet until you reach a road sign left for Porthallow. Here you will notice an acorn sign by a metal gate - this field path short-cuts a big road bend but eventually you have to walk the tarmac for about 500m - shady for most of the way - into **PORTHALLOW** *(tea-rooms; pub; small shop; accommodation; telephone; car parking; toilets)*.

Somewhat off the beaten track for most tourists, Porthallow has a sheltered, shingly beach popular with boat owners. The village bought its foreshore as an amenity and car parking is allowed there for the price of a voluntary donation.

Porthallow

SECTION 4 - Porthallow to Falmouth;   15 miles (24km)

Flowery slopes offering wide coastal views precede creekside and riverside walking (including a low-tide wade or taking to country lanes) to Helford for the river passenger ferry. Once across, the route follows a very pleasant course back seaward, passing wooded inlets and rocky promontories before rounding Rosemullion Head to Maenporth Beach. Another mile of high level walking brings you to Swanpool Beach and either a circumvention of Pendennis Head or a direct road entry to Falmouth.   Grading - moderate. Refreshments, shop and accommodation at Helford. Refreshments, limited accommodation at Helford Passage. Refreshments at Maenporth (seasonal).

Walk along Porthallow's diminutive seafront and climb steps at the far end past private houses up to densely vegetated clifftop. Soon you are out along field edges above flowery hillside with marvellous views towards Falmouth and beyond to Dodman Point in clear conditions. After a stone stile and finger post, aim obliquely down right to a step-stile in the field's seaward corner. (It may be necessary to improvise here owing to the deployment of electric fencing.)

The coast path goes right round Nare Point as a track serving the

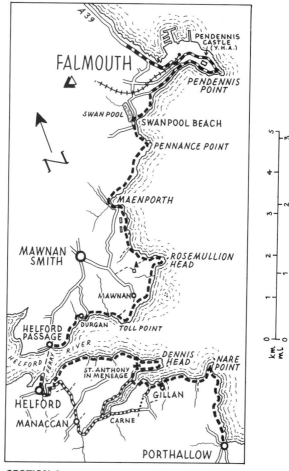

SECTION 4
PORTHALLOW to FALMOUTH

Coastguard lookout, all the while becoming more riverside in character. Follow it past Parbean Cove, but where the track swings left
inland in woods, turn right over a footbridge. Dennis Head is seen
over to the right across the mouth of Gillan Creek as the way undulates

past Mên-aver Point. Coming to a large hilltop property on the left, turn right down steps past a small inlet to emerge at **GILLAN HARBOUR.** Cross the stream footbridge and continue up the enclosed path past a long white house and out to the country road-end at Flushing Cove.

The many-creeked Helford River which drains the 'Meneage' (the so-called 'Land of Monks' south of the river where several monasteries were established prior to the Norman Conquest and which is characterised by lush woodland, rich farms and winding, flowery lanes) presents east-bound walkers with their first obstacle to progress. There are further river crossings to come on the South Cornwall and South Devon coast paths, some simpler than others. All require some deliberate strategy to avoid frustration - this mainly involves awareness of tides, weather conditions and ferry operating times. Tide timetables are widely available in shops and are included in the South West Way Association's annual handbook.

Gillan Creek now separates us from St. Anthony-in-Meneage and the path round Dennis Head to Helford. You have 3 options: first to wade the creek, second to walk on country lanes to Carne and thence by creekside road to St. Anthony, third to tramp the roads direct to Helford via Manaccan.

Near the Helford Ferry

Helford Passage

OPTION A (the official route): Wading Gillan Creek is only possible our hour either side of low water, so either plan your arrival to coincide with appropriate tide times, or be prepared to wait!

From Flushing Cove, stay on the creekside path - recently reinstated after landslip - until you can go no further. Steps lead down to the beach and the best course over the water channel is directly towards two old caravans (failing this, try 200 yards further upstream). On the other side turn right and join the lane past 15th century St. Anthony's church, where the footpath continues out round Dennis Head through the Bosahan Estate. This private path (no dogs) is not cleared as regularly as one would hope for but soon reaches open ground round the headland - a superb spot from which to watch shipping offshore as well as pleasure craft in the estuary. From here you hug the southern shore of the Helford River, first through fields then in and out of woods to the road at Treath where you come inland a little and drop to **HELFORD** *(accommodation; tea gardens; pub; Post Office/General Store; telephone; car park; toilets)*, a one-time smugglers' haunt, now famed for its sailing and oysters.

OPTION B: If Gillan Creek is marginally too deep to wade, you could try crossing about 200m further upstream. Otherwise retrace steps past Halamana Cottage and turn right up the lane, keeping ahead on a path off the left bend to reach the road near Gillywartha Farm. Turn right down to Carne and right again to cross the creek, now following the lane along Gillan Creek's northern shore for a mile to St. Anthony. Here pick up the official route described in Option A.

OPTION C: Follow Option B to Carne but keep straight on along the shady riverside road, bearing right up to Manaccan *(pub; shop; Post Office/ Store; telephone)*. Continue north, crossing the main Helston road and in 750m turn sharp left down past a car park to Helford.

All options having now converged, walk over the creek footbridge and turn right along the narrow lane past picturesque cottages, the Post Office, tea gardens and pub, forking right through a gate/step-stile for the footpath to Helford Ferry.

The licensed ferry to Helford Passage runs from Good Friday to October 31st, 9.00am. to 5.30pm. - frequency depends on demand and is subject to tide and weather conditions (strong winds can produce rough seas). Outside this operational period, a ferry service is offered by the Helford Boatyard (tel: Manaccan 5823 232) - again subject to tide and sea. At the author's last visit, the ferry cafe (a welcome place to await a crossing) was sadly no longer in business. Even so, time can be spent pleasantly enough watching the activities in this popular waterway, providing the weather if favourable.

Disembarking at **HELFORD PASSAGE** *(pub; cafe; telephone; toilets)*, take the footpath from the east end of the river frontage, signed 'Durgan'. This leads you straightforwardly along by bushes above the estuary and out onto a surfaced track. Keep right, outside Durgan Gardens fence, to weave beneath an arch and up steps, regaining the river bank through trees and down into **DURGAN** *(telephone; NO parking!)*. At a finger post, turn sharp right along by pretty cottages in this sleepy and wooded National Trust hamlet.

Walk up the tarmac access lane with fine river views and where it swings left at the top, cross a stone stile by the gate ahead (signed 'Bosloe'). The path lies along the seaward edge of pasture, eventually dropping past a path left (up the Carwinion Valley) to a slipway. Go along the back of the little beach and up past a wartime gun position before arriving at the next small cove - Porthallack. Pass a shack there, cross the brook and a path left to Mawnan and enter the National Trust's Mawnan Glebe property round Toll Point.

From a navigation marker there are wide views back to Dennis Head and the lookout on Nare Point across the Helford estuary, as the path climbs and enters woods at Mawnan Shear. Fork right on a broad path (left leads to Mawnan hamlet in 200m - 15th century church, car parking), down through delightful woodland above Parson's Beach, ending in steps up and a stile out the other side onto bushy clifftops.

The coast path crosses wheat fields in a straight line above vast rock platforms on the foreshore, before swinging east (beware concealed holes in the ground) out round **ROSEMULLION HEAD.** This is another exciting corner of coastline, with Falmouth and St. Anthony Head lighthouse revealed and even a distant glimpse of The Lizard still possible to the south-west. The dangerously crumbling cliff edge on Rosemullion Head is best kept well back from, whereafter the way climbs round an inlet to a gate/stile. *(Straight on - west - passes a trig. pillar into a lane and continues by road to Mawnan Smith village - 1 mile. Pub; accommodation; Post Office; telephone; buses for Falmouth.)*

You now fork right across a field with almost more bluebells than grass in May, towards the houses of Meuden. Keep to the right-hand trod, cross a stream at the bottom (path up left to Mawnan Smith) and the hotel path just beyond, and climb the field ahead. Once over a stile you are walking along half-way up between hilltop properties and the rocky shore of The Hutches. Threading pleasantly through vegetation outside private gardens, the coast path emerges along a field, protected from its unstable seaward edge by chain link fencing.

A rusting wreck can be spotted jammed under the cliffs opposite as you turn into the deep bay of **MAENPORTH** *(summer cafe at each end; pub in the middle; car parking; toilets).* Follow the road round to the far (north) end of the beach and turn right by the toilets on the well walked coast path which climbs and falls gently for a mile or so on high hillside round Newporth Head and Pennance Point. From here a wooded track leads down to the road at Swanpool Beach *(nearby campsite; cafes; pub; beach shops; car park; toilets).*

We have now effectively reached **FALMOUTH** *(all shops and services; accommodation, including youth hostel on Pendennis Point; pubs, cafes and restaurants; BR station; buses; hospital; museum; tourist inform-ation; car parks; toilets; early closing Wednesday).* Should a direct line to the shops and amenities be required, follow the road along the east bank of Swan Pool, turn right then left and continue ahead down to the main harbour-front shopping street (about 1½ miles - 2.5km).

If, however, there is time to spare, a waterfront circumvention of Pendennis Point will provide the finest perspectives of Falmouth and its great natural anchorage of Carrick Roads. A surfaced path leads onward from Swanpool Beach round to Gyllyngvase Beach (short-cut left over to the harbour area), where you pick up the seafront road right out to Pendennis Point.

Pendennis Castle and its sister fortress at St. Mawes across the water

are exceptionally good examples of the south coast harbour fortifications instigated by Henry VIII in 1539 on an Italian design. Both
were started in 1542 to protect Falmouth's deep water anchorage
which had eclipsed Penryn as the west's major sea port, not least for
the export of tin from local mines. Even so, Falmouth Harbour itself
was a modest affair until around 1860 when the present complex had
begun to be built. A century ago, Carrick Roads and the channel
leading to Penryn often contained several hundred sailing ships lying
at anchor; such vessels would bear the brunt of easterly gales to which
the seaway is exposed.

Falmouth was a mail packet station from 1688 until the mid-19th
century when steam power led to this service being transferred to
Southampton. As a cargo port, Falmouth's fortunes have waxed and
waned with market forces and although the sizeable docks are not as
busy as they once were, the town plays host to large numbers of
summer visitors, also remaining a shopping and commercial centre for
the surrounding rural area.

SECTION 5 - Falmouth to Portscatho;   6 miles (10km)

*A short day in mileage terms but complicated by the need for catching ferries
and finding the best way to reach the resumption of the coast path proper at
Place Manor. Thereafter, the shores of Carrick Roads lead out round St.
Anthony Head and Zone Point past the lighthouse and old gun position,
affording excellent views of shipping and pleasure boats in the estuary. The
undulating path then threads along the edge of fields above sheer cliffs and
past a couple of unspoiled sandy beaches, finally entering the small harbour
resort of Portscatho.   Grading - moderate.*
Shops, services and accommodation at St. Mawes.

NOTE: The onward coast path from Falmouth resumes at Place
Manor on the Roseland Peninsula - the other side of Carrick Roads!
Getting there, it cannot be denied, is something of a headache! Even if
you have motor transport and are walking day stages, the drive round
via the A39, King Harry Ferry and Portscatho is considerable. If you
are on foot, crossing to St. Mawes by ferry is simple but the Percuil
River, which splits Roseland into two fingers, separates you tantalis-
ingly from Place Manor and the coast path. It is the kind of situation
which calls for individual initiative and lateral thinking, but the more
obvious options are set out below!

OPTION A: (the most satisfactory if it can be arranged): Enquire at
Falmouth's Prince of Wales Pier to obtain transport across Carrick

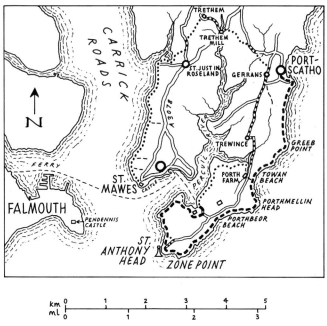

SECTION 5
FALMOUTH to PORTSCATHO

Roads direct to the slipway at Place Manor. This will, of course, depend on tide, weather and sea conditions being favourable.

OPTION B: (second best if it can be arranged): Catch the ferry to St. Mawes from Prince of Wales Pier (in summer - half-hourly weekdays, hourly Sundays. In winter - 5 boats daily, no Sunday service. Ferry subject to weather and sea conditions). The St. Mawes Ferry Co. will land parties of 20 or more at Place Manor provided this is arranged in advance - subject to weather, tide and sea conditions. Otherwise, individual enquiries can be made at St. Mawes to procure someone willing to take you across the Percuil River to Place Manor.

It is naturally to be hoped that a realistic level of remuneration will be offered by walkers to any kind soul in the boating fraternity who is able to help. That way, future walkers are more likely to meet with positive responses to their own enquiries.

OPTION C: Cross to St. Mawes by ferry as in Option B and hire a taxi to drive you round to Place Manor via Portscatho - about 8 miles (13km) and not too expensive if you are a small group. Alternatively try hitching a lift all or part of the way!

OPTION D: (for purists!): Cross to St. Mawes by ferry and walk! If you don't mind a road-bash (the most direct route), take the A3078 past St. Just in Roseland and Trethem Mill where you cross the Percuil River. About 800m up the hill beyond, turn sharp right and follow this by-road, turning right through Gerrans (Portscatho on your left) and continuing via Tregassick and Trewince to Froe. Soon after you will see a sign right 'Footpath to Place by Percuil River'. Cross the creek's footbridge here and keep along the river shore round to Place Manor.

Tempted by the coast path's proximity at Portscatho, many long-distance walkers elect to forego the St. Anthony Head circuit in favour of straightforward easterly progress. However, the St. Anthony Peninsula is a marvellous, unspoilt stretch of coastline to explore - free from crowds, offering superb sea views and with a couple of secluded beaches.

NOTE: If you would like to walk from St. Mawes but are discouraged from doing so by the prospect of tramping along a main road, a more circuitous and undoubtedly more enjoyable routing is available. It takes in St. Mawes Castle (an architectural gem of the Tudor period), follows the Carrick Roads shoreline to St. Just in Roseland and uses rights of way to Trethem and Trethem Mill where a final footpath route leads up through woods and out to the by-road near Gerrans. Thereafter follow the directions above to Place Manor. This is not an 'official' stretch of path, but has been researched and recommended by the South West Way Association - detailed directions to it appear in their annual South West Way handbook.

Standing on the site of a 13th century monastery building, **PLACE MANOR** is an imposing edifice, its vast lawns a filled-in tide power mill pond which served the local people for 3 centuries. From the creek slipway, walk up the lane for some 300m and turn right at a sign and stile. Old tombstones lead to St.Anthony-in-Roseland parish church, little changed since the 12th and 13th centuries. Passing its Norman doorway, you walk up left where waymarks lead to a wide track. Turn down right then left at the bottom on a shady track round the Percuil River shore, with delightful views out to pleasure craft and nearby St. Mawes.

Opposite the entrance to a little river beach, turn left up a field to the top stile and prepare yourself for a stunning panorama across Carrick Roads, from St. Mawes to Pendennis castles, Falmouth

St.Anthony-in-Roseland

Docks and a great deal of shipping activity.

From the stile, walk left outside a field hedge, either keeping down along the seaward edge of a hilly field at Carricknath Point and climbing to a stand of Scots pines, or taking the higher level short-cut. Both paths soon converge and, with **ST. ANTHONY HEAD** lighthouse now clear ahead, the way reaches a footbridge over a boggy stream mouth.

Again there are 2 minor options: Climb direct to the car park and turn right through it towards the headland. Or, more pleasantly, go right from the stream (waymarked), past the lighthouse's one-time paraffin store and turn sharp left up steps just before the lighthouse itself.

At the top where both alternatives join, turn right past a row of cottages to the old St. Anthony Battery. Along with Pendennis and St. Mawes, this defended Falmouth for 60 years and as recently as 1956 (3 years before it was acquired by the National Trust) the battery was fully operational with ammunition, communications systems and weapons all in place. An explanatory diagram has been put up next to the toilets.

A viewing table interestingly points out features to look for, given reasonable visibility, then the path swings north-east round **ZONE**

Towan Beach

POINT on pleasant, gorsey clifftops. From here to Mevagissey, 24 miles (39km) distant, the coastline is largely unspoiled and surprisingly little frequented - largely due to its being off the main tourist routes and having no major resorts. However, thanks to the National Trust, the path is well maintained and there is a marvellous diversity of coastal scenery, from secluded beaches to rugged headlands. Though demanding effort at times and offering fewer refreshment points, the walking is some of the best on the entire south coast.

Past Porthbeor Beach sands *(limited verge parking on nearby lane)*, you are skirting the edges of large grain fields, remote from the hustle and bustle of Cornwall's holiday scene. A great, slanting cleft above Elwinick Cove precedes crossing the neck of Porthmellin Head, with the unmistakable bulk of Nare Head now on the near horizon.

From Killigerran Head, a sweep of bay brings you past a white rocket post to **TOWAN BEACH** *(National Trust car park at Porth Farm, 5 minutes by easy path inland)*. With no facilities at all, the beach of coarse sand and shingle backed by dunes and low cliffs is never crowded and will appeal to those attracted by 'getting away from it all!'

Cross the beach access track and walk along the low cliffs; beyond, gentle undulations belie the dangerously overhanging edge in places. Past Greeb Point you will pass a path up left to a caravan/campsite and access, right, to a tiny beach. Soon a gate and stile finally lead down a tarmac path to the road and buildings of **PORTSCATHO** *(shop; pub; cafe/restaurant; accommodation, including campsite at top of hill;*

telephone; car parking; toilets), originally a fishing village and now a quiet holiday retreat. The Plume of Feathers pub dates from the 17th century.

SECTION 6 - Portscatho to Gorran Haven;   15 miles (24km)

An increasingly strenuous day over rougher terrain, more remote and less well endowed with accommodation places. Allow about 7 hours actual walking time. Inhabited, low cliffs lead to the mile-long Pendower Beach and the start of stiffer gradients as you cross Nare Head, with magnificent views. Close to cliff edge indentations, the path reaches the tiny, select village of Portloe and continues with some steep but not sustained climbs to the little beach hamlet of Portholland. Passing a late-17th century castle and popular Porthluney Cove sands, the way traverses wild and rugged

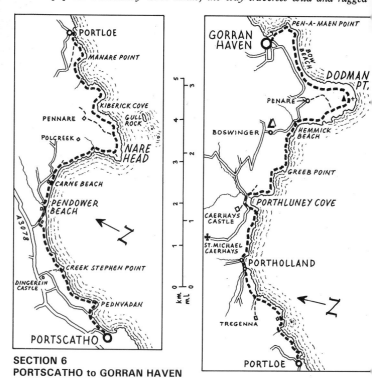

SECTION 6
PORTSCATHO to GORRAN HAVEN

70

Portscatho

coastline to another sandy bay and an ascent of the Dodman - a major headland. Gradually dropping round field edges above a shingle bay, a final promontory is mounted to gain the harbour and old fishing village of Gorran Haven. Grading - moderate at first, becoming more difficult; strenuous here and there.

Drinks, snacks and accommodation at Pendower Beach. Drinks, meals and some accommodation, also Post Office/Stores at Portloe. Post Office/Stores and seasonal refreshments at East Portholland. Drinks and snacks at Porthluney Cove. Youth hostel near Hemmick Sands.

Leave Porthscatho on the seaward street running north and pick up the coast path to Porthcurnick Beach *(seasonal cafe/beach shop)*. Rounding Pednvadan headland with its Coastguard lookout and fine retrospective views over Portscatho, the way undulates above modest cliffs past salubrious hotels inland, dropping to the beach at Porthbean. Copses of low, scrubby trees and bushes lead on to another descent to a stream at Creek Stephen Point (path up left to the large, tree-covered mound known as Dingerein Castle, reputedly once belonging to Geraint, the 8th century Cornish king and saint).

2km farther on there is a diversion up left to pass behind the Pendower Hotel (rather than across its grounds!). Turn right down the road *(parking)* to popular **PENDOWER BEACH** *(hotel offering coffees, light lunches and cream teas, also beer garden).*

Nare Head

From here to Gorran Haven, the going becomes noticeably more strenuous and progress will be slower on the often tortuous path. To begin with, however, cross the stream and walk along the back of Pendower Beach to the little country road *(toilets)*. Turn right and in 20m right again over a stile, now above a long stretch of safe bathing sands to Carne Beach. Passing seaward of tennis courts at Nare Hotel, turn right when you meet the road *(car parking);* note the wartime bunker converted to a bungalow's outhouse. In 50m turn right through a gate and proceed ahead along the edge of rough pasture. It is well worth glancing back, for views extend round Gerrans Bay and far beyond to the Helford River mouth and Lowlands Point.

At first the onward path meanders easily along despite less cultivated surroundings, but soon more determined legwork is called for to cross the stream valley below Polcreek. There ensues a steady pull up past a small ruin and a path off left, the gradient then steepening to a waymark post (especially useful in poor visibility). You now aim for the headland's top; a strategically placed bench under a rock outcrop provides unsurpassed coastal views as you rise to the 330ft. (100m) crest of **NARE HEAD.**

Keeping left of the gorse (no obvious path initially), you will soon pick up a farm track leading to a National Trust car park. (By going seaward of the gorse on one of several thin trods, you obtain good prospects of Gull Rock and its seabird colonies but have to fight back inland through the dense, prickly bushes.) At the car park, head ½-right for the stile in the far clifftop corner.

Unseen before, Veryan Bay unfolds dramatically, ending in the Dodman, notorious for its shipwrecks. Also visible are the 'Cornish Alps' - heaps of china-clay waste on the horizon near St. Austell; the industry will be encountered closer at hand further along the path. Succeeding headlands like Nare Head are coastal equivalents to cols or saddles in mountain country, each one offering new and surprising vistas of fresh territory.

The coast path now makes a big curve inland round the elegant valley behind Kiberick Cove and walkers are asked not to short-cut straight across. *(For access to Pennare and the National Trust car park, keep left for 200m.)* Continuing round the edge of fields past Parc Caragloose, a new, well-made section of path avoids the old flight of 70-odd very steep steps to sea level. The rocky cliff line is closely hugged round Manare and Jacka points and abruptly you arrive at **PORTLOE** *(inn; hotel; limited accommodation; Post Office/Stores; telephone).*

A considerably more affluent place than a century ago when it struggled for existence as a fishing hamlet, Portloe might strike the muddy, trail-worn coastal walker today as a trifle over prettified and exclusive. An off-the-beaten-track destination for motorists and a retreat for the well-to-do and retired, it seems to lack that essential warmth which welcomes everyone, whatever their status.

Steps past the Lugger Hotel lead up to a Coastguard lookout, whereafter the path stays close to the edge of sheer cliffs, crossing a stream and rounding the minor promontory of Caragloose Point, with Shag Rock just offshore.

A stiff little climb past an isolated house and there is somewhat easier ground ahead down to the track from Tregenna *(campsite).* Another rise inland is taken, cutting Perbargus Point, and you come down to the road at West Portholland by the old Methodist chapel (still used). Walk ahead up the subsidence-prone road and turn off right to the quiet cove of **EAST PORTHOLLAND** *(Post Office/ Stores; sometime seasonal refreshments at nearby house; small car park; toilets).*

Following round the concrete beach top and gently shelving sands, the route continues past a finger post as a tarmac pathway climbing back to the clifftops (path off left to St. Michael Caerhays church). This promising path eventually fizzles out at a field, where you turn right, skirting its seaward perimeter past a ruinous Coastguard look-

Caerhays Castle and Porthluney Cove

out. Emerging onto a shady lane, turn down right and note Caerhays Castle to your left in its impressive grounds (open to the public but one day a year!). Constructed by John Nash in 1808 on the site of an old manor house, the building is best seen from a few hundred metres ahead.

PORTHLUNEY COVE *(beach shop/cafe - packed lunches, pasties, cream teas; large grassy car park; toilets)* is very popular in summer. Just beyond the castle's main entrance, the coast path turns off right, up round fields and keeping to the seaward of two diverging trods. From the cliff edge above the beach are the most favourable castle views.

Once the climbing is done here, the path contours along bushy hilltop through the odd copse or thicket, with glimpses far back west towards The Lizard in clear conditions. After a substantial drop over a stream valley above inaccessible Lambsowden Cove near Greeb Point, the way grows more sinuous and rocky, winding in and out, up and down, through low scrub with a distinctly more remote ambience.

The next sandy bay - **HEMMICK BEACH** - is soon approached on a gentle descent over grassy fields *(very limited parking; no facilities; 800m up road to left is Boswinger youth hostel with family rooms)*. Walk ahead up the road for about 25m and turn up right at a National Trust sign for the Dodman. (NOTE:In poor weather or pressing circumstances, stay on the road for a short-cut across the neck of the Dodman

Hemmick Beach (distant left) and Dodman Point

to Gorran Haven via Penare hamlet.)

Following the initial steep climb, the path eases off pleasantly through bracken above Gell and High points, with extensive views as one would expect from such a prominent headland. A further climb brings you to a handgate (left to Penare, ½ mile) where the coast path turns right, outside a field fence along to **DODMAN POINT**. Its huge granite cross, erected in 1896 on the instigation of the rector of St. Michael Caerhays, is topped by a very necessary lightning conductor! Dodman (literally Dead Man) and the treacherous coast north to Black Head have seen more than their fair share of shipwrecks.

There is a triangulation pillar in the gorse just inland, but the coast path takes off down to the right, swinging north along the clifftops with magnificent views ahead. Conspicuous is the red and white day mark on Gribbin Head across St. Austell Bay. Rame Head and sometimes even Bolt Tail are visible in the far distance.

More field edges lead on round the long shingle strand of Bow, or Vault, Beach (which is reached from the far end at Cadythew Rock where the cliffs are lowest). A modest, scrambly climb over Pen-a-maen Point past a Coastguard lookout brings you down to the south end of **GORRAN HAVEN** *(food and gift shops; pub; cafes; accommodation; Post Office; telephone; car park; toilets; boats for hire; occasional buses for Mevagissey and St. Austell).*

The granite cross on Dodman Point

Sheltered from the south-west by flanking hills and swelled by much new building, Gorran Haven seems uncomfortably squeezed into its valley. The sandy beach is well patronised in summer but is not particularly attractive and walkers are more likely to be interested in the village's old narrow streets up from the harbour.

SECTION 7 - Gorran Haven to Par;   13 miles (21km)

Pleasant clifftop walking to the lively fishing harbour of Mevagissey. A short walk to the next bay, after which there are some stiff gradients to contend with as the path rounds Black Head and reaches the little industrial port of Charlestown. Increasingly built-up and much easier walking, you pass close to hotels, the 'Cornish Leisure World' complex, main railway line and a large golf course before approaching a big china-clay works at Par Harbour. An unavoidable stretch of road leads round to the town of Par with its sands and seafront caravan park.   Grading - moderate, but more difficult between Mevagissey and Porthpean.

Seasonal pub at Portmellon. Most shops, services and accommodation at

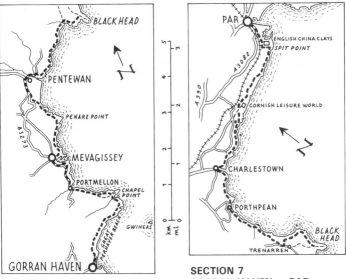

SECTION 7
GORRAN HAVEN to PAR

Mevagissey. Shop, pub, cafes and accommodation at Pentewan. Seasonal refreshments at Porthpean. Shop, pub, cafe/restaurant at Charlestown. Meals and drinks at Cornish Leisure World just off-route.

To leave Gorran Haven, walk up Church Street past the tiny chapel of St. Just and turn right along Cliff Road (cul-de-sac) past houses. At the road end, a stile leads into fields high above Great Perhaver Beach.

A mile offshore lie the Gwineas Rocks, responsible for many shipwrecks. Notable among them were the brig 'Brandywine Packet' in January 1838 with the loss of all but one of the crew; the 1,350 ton Russian barque 'Pallas' in November 1895 which subsequently drove onto Perhaver Beach with no casualties; and the 5,200 ton steamer 'Ardangorm' which struck the reef on January 4th 1940 and remains there to this day, though much salvaged and lying in deep water.

The path continues straightforwardly, descending to Turbot Point and over a stream leading to Colona Beach. Houses on Chapel Point, put up speculatively in the 1930's, have a distinctly 'un-English' appearance! Following a field round west, you soon emerge on a private road down to **PORTMELLON** *(just a cluster of houses, a seasonal pub and a one-time busy boatyard now overwhelmed by building development).*

77

Gorran Haven

Owing to the funnelling effect of this narrow bay, waves are pushed up higher than normal by an incoming tide and the little seafront is often flooded. The author vividly recalls a summer holiday spent in one of the seafront houses when only stout shutters prevented crashing waves and pebbles from inundating the rooms, downstairs and up!

Unfortunately, the onward route is forced onto the busy road for ¾ mile (1,200m), but you can avoid the last bit by walking through a small park area before descending into **MEVAGISSEY** *(shops, services and accommodation; pubs, cafes and restaurants; Post Office; telephones; buses for St. Austell; car park; toilets; Aquarium; boat trips, including shark fishing! model railway exhibition; early closing Wednesday).*

Although this is still one of Cornwall's busiest fishing ports, its heyday was probably around the end of the last century before the great pilchard shoals dwindled due to climatic changes and the southwest's fishing industry went into decline. Today Mevagissey manages to go about its business - as the working harbour will testify - but it seems in danger of becoming swamped by tourists in the summer months. Nevertheless its fascinating waterfront and double harbour provide a welcome change of scene for the coastal walker: as fishing villages go, it ranks as one of the liveliest.

From the north end of the quayside, walk up the narrow lane past picturesque cottages, rising above the harbour and out round near a Coastguard station. Continuing past houses and a playing field, the cliff path undulates round Penare Point, along field edges and down to

The Harbour, Mevagissey

Portgiskey where it runs first above, then alongside, the B3273, finally joining it behind the vast flat caravan and camping ground at Pentewan Beach. Stay on the road and turn right, over the river and along to the small harbour at **PENTEWAN** *(shops; pub; cafes; restaurant; some accommodation; Post Office; telephone; car park; toilets)*.

Cross the stream by the road bridge and walk up the road for 100m before turning sharp right at a sign 'To the Church' and 'The Terrace'. Go along this drive, past the church and fork left up between wire fences past a notice not to trespass on Polrudden Cliffs and fields. Copious barbed wire makes a mockery of such a request and serves as a reminder of the sometimes aggressive attitude shown by landowners in granting access to the public. Even if the barbed wire detracts a little from a full sense of freedom while walking these fine cliffs, the routing is infinitely preferable to the previous inland diversion on roads through Trenarren.

There are several sizeable down-and-ups, mostly now equipped with timber steps where there were once muddy scrambles. A boggy stream has a footbridge but if the path is overgrown, beware nasty holes in the ground on the next ascent.

Topping a rise, Par Sands appear ahead, with Black Head over to the right and much closer now. The descent to Hallane Mill Cove is through lovely wild woods. Once over the stream footbridge, turn right and at the next stream in an idyllic little glen, a path goes down right, past a house to the diminutive beach - a superb picnic spot.

The coast path, however, swings up left here and 20m beyond a gate turns right (straight on is a short-cut to roadside parking at Trenarren, missing the walk round Black Head and Gerrans Point). After the next stiff ascent, the path meanders through gorse and wild flowers towards **BLACK HEAD,** a wonderful viewpoint in good weather and accessible to the right at the next path junction. The onward coast path forks sharp left here between thorn bushes and past an over-grown lookout up to a finger post, where it veers rights.

Ahead the still beautiful coast is fringed with rocky coves and clifftop houses and hotels around Porthpean on the outskirts of St. Austell. Charlestown harbour is visible, as is sandy Carlyon Bay and the big china-clay works on Spit Point.

Reaching a waymark post, turn down right and at a bench turn up left through pleasant woodland to meet a stony track (left is a short-cut to Black Head). Turning right past a derelict building, you will soon come out to a minor road *(car parking)*, a short distance along which, watch for the path forking off right over a stile. It threads along the seaward edges of fields, still hemmed in by the ubiquitous barbed wire, goes steeply down above an inaccessible cove, crosses a small footbridge and climbs equally steeply up. At the next stile, keep right down the field edge then up again, finally descending on an enclosed path to the road end and slipway opposite to the yacht club at **PORTHPEAN** *(summer refreshment hut; toilets)*.

The beach is sandy shingle but cliffs each end are dangerously unstable. Walk along the miniature promenade and go left up steps to a tarmac path outside private gardens. It is shady, easy going - keep straight ahead at a junction - and continues in the same vein along the clifftops, cutting across Carrickowel Point and eventually going round by a wall and down to **CHARLESTOWN** *(cafe/gift shop; restaurant; pub; Post Office/Store up road; some buses for St. Austell; car park; toilets; Visitor Centre)*.

A small industrial port named after Charles Rashleigh from Menabilly, near Fowey, who built it around 1790, Charlestown was originally intended to handle ore from nearby mines. However, china-clay soon began to dominate cargoes, although Par and Fowey were ultimately to become more important to the industry and Charlestown fell into a semi-slumber. Only recent changes in ownership seem likely to drag the community reluctantly - and rather regrettably - into the late 20th century. Its authenticity and lack of modern development have made Charlestown a destination for student field trips and curious holiday-makers alike. Scenes from the 'Onedin Line' and 'Voyage of the Beagle' were filmed here. In 1971 the dock entrance was widened and a new gate fitted - if not in use, it is over this gate which you now walk.

Go forward past the toilets, up a field edge and through a copse. At a path junction with handgates, keep right, perhaps giving a backwards glance to Black Head and the coastline just traversed.

You will emerge at a road opposite the Porth Avallen Hotel and stay alongside it for 100m before dropping along vegetated clifftops, once again outside the boundaries of private properties. Keep ahead over an open area of short cropped grass past the huge Carlyon Bay Hotel and skirt a vast car park, witness to the popularity of this bay. Cross the access road to the 'Entertainment Capital of the West - Cornish Leisure World' - a warehouse-like complex which includes a 'fun pub', video games, Wimpy Bar, miniature railway, fish and chips, ice-cream and a swimming pool, as well as night club, roller disco and 2,500 seat auditorium.

The coast path continues along the cliffs above a broad sandy beach, with golf links and the main railway line to your left. After some distance there is a loop down right but you are soon back by the golf

Charlestown Harbour Entrance

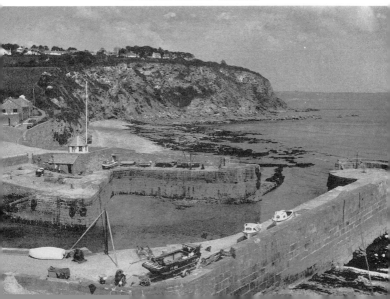

The path through English China Clays

course, which now extends right down to **SPIT POINT**. Seen from afar and now approached are the shining aluminium chimneys of English China Clays' major works. Fine white dust is blown across a large area and undergrowth is coated with a false frost.

From Spit Point a tarmac path runs inland (north-west) between chain link fencing next to the installations. A footbridge spans road-ways past monolithic silos and steaming networks of pipes. Before a fairly recent extension to this concessionary path, the routing went left under the railway to the road and at the author's last visit a finger post still pointed that way. Keep walking along by the works perimeter however, alongside the railway as far as the main Harbour Office entrance. From here it is a short road bash, turning right at some shops onto the Fowey road (A3082) and entering **PAR** *(all shops, services and accommodation; buses for Fowey and St. Austell; British Rail main line station; car park; toilets; early closing Thursday).*

SECTION 8 - Par to Looe;   16 miles (26km)

Leaving Par's industrial installations behind, there is good cliff walking to picturesque Polkerris and on round Gribbin Head. Past coves and an orna-mental lake, the sheltered anchorage and yachting town of Fowey is reached. A passenger ferry takes you across the river to the start of 6 miles (10km) of wild and much more remote coastline, quite strenuous in places but wonderfully unspoiled. Polperro, the archetypal Cornish fishing village, is often crowded in summer but there is a good onward cliff path to Talland Bay Beach, then further delightful walking on grassy hillside above the sea to West Looe. Along with East Looe, this is a sizeable town with all amenities, a lively harbour and a popular beach.   Grading -mostly moderate but more difficult between Polruan and Polperro.

Pub and cafe at Polkerris. All shops, services and accommodation (including Youth Hostel) at Fowey. Refreshments at Polruan. Pubs and eating places and shops at Polperro. Seasonal refreshments at Talland Beach.

To leave Par, either walk along the beach or the ramped campsite roadway behind the dunes, to the east of the beach. At the car park there, keep ahead over a small footbridge and turn right up steps onto the coast path atop low cliffs. (A less appealing alternative is the main road parallel to the beach from Par Green, turning right onto the path at Polmear.)

Par Sands are extensive at low tide and the mere just east of the campsite is a good place for birdwatching. Apart from coasters waiting to enter Par harbour, there is soon little to remind you of the industry which dominates this corner of south Cornwall. Indeed, ahead lies an area of outstanding natural beauty and much more superlative coastal walking to Plymouth.

Inside a field fence on a sometimes narrow path, you quickly arrive at charming **POLKERRIS** *(cafe; pub; boats for hire; toilets).* The

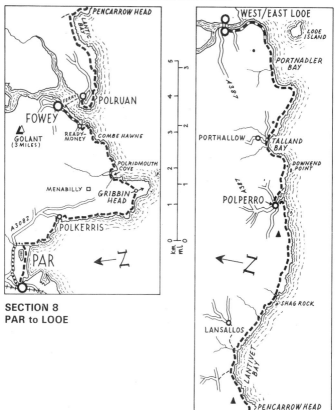

SECTION 8
PAR to LOOE

restored and much ornamented Rashleigh Arms resembles an interesting museum as much as a pub; the tiny harbour and small beach are quite unspoiled.

Turn right to the road end and beach, then left to a coast path sign and steps. Zig-zags follow, up through delightful woods, the air heavy with wild garlic, until a stile brings you out onto open cliffs again with excellent views back over Par's docks to Black Head. Staying along the cliff edge, there is a climb through gorse to a stile, whereafter the rather overgrown path leads easily out to a change of direction on the Little Gribbin.

Rounding badly eroded clifftops, the way passes behind an old overgrown field wall and there are sudden exciting views of the coast ahead. Keep right, past a National Trust sign and soon you come round to confront the 80ft. (25m) tall, square, red and white striped navigation day mark on **GRIBBIN HEAD**, erected in 1832 by Trinity House.

As you drop over a stile and field towards Polridmouth Cove, Fowey's drowned river valley - or 'ria' - lies directly ahead. The route keeps right, round the cove *(no motor access, refreshments or facilities but safe bathing)* and beyond a house goes along a low, concrete dam forming a small ornamental lake with swans which is flanked by immaculate lawns. (½ mile inland is Menabilly, seat of the Rashleigh family of Charlestown fame, and for some years home of the author Daphne du Maurier). Past the stream outlet, keep ahead up steps, over a stile and out onto clifftop fields. Cross a big wall stile and walk down pasture above bramble and gorse-covered cliffs.

Before reaching Fowey, the sizeable inlet of Combe Hawne has to be negotiated, involving a drop to sea level and subsequent climb. Farther on, a stone tablet commemorates the donation of fields to the people of Fowey.

Through a kissing gate, you descend a woodland path down left over smoothed rocks, turning right at the junction with Lovers Lane and reaching the road at Readymoney hamlet. Follow the lane ahead

Fowey from the ferry to Polruan

which leads directly into **FOWEY** - pronounced 'Foy' - *(all shops, services and accommodation; youth hostel at Golant; buses to Par and St. Austell; passenger ferry to Polruan; car ferry to Bodinnick; museum; early closing Wednesday).*

In 1380, Fowey was raided by a large Spanish fleet and to deter further would-be enemies, a great chain was stretched between two blockhouses at the harbour entrance; only the Polruan one remains. Fowey has a long and illustrious maritime history which its museum elucidates. During the 19th century, shipbuilding and the export of ores and china-clay were thriving and even as recently as the Second World War Fowey's harbour was still active as a base for rescue services and American forces on D-Day. Today, English China Clays export some 1.6 million tonnes to all parts of the world; their dock for ocean-going ships is connected to Par by private road to avoid pollution of the town. Even so, the predominant usage and enjoyment of Fowey's sheltered anchorage is by pleasure craft which frequent both the river and offshore waters.

The passenger ferry across the River Fowey to Polruan runs every 10 to 15 minutes in summer, from early in the day till late. It leaves from a jetty reached down an alley off the road just south-west of the town centre, but in the winter may operate from the town quay.

The ensuing 6 miles (10km) to Polperro should not be undertaken too casually, for the walking is strenuous along remote coastline devoid of habitation, let alone refreshment points! Although narrow at times, the path is clear all the way, largely thanks to the National Trust, and the coastal scenery is outstanding.

Walk up **POLRUAN'S** main street for a few metres *(nearby pubs, a few shops and cafe)* then turn right, signed 'Footpath to Cliffs'. Follow these signs along above good harbour views and keep ahead at a cul-de-sac sign. The lane narrows to a path and emerges on the cliffs by a Coastguard lookout.

Turn up left, then swing right as the path levels off past the stump of an old tower and meets the road by a school. (Alternative access to here is via Polruan's Fore Street.) Turn sharp right at the next road junction and down the coast path towards Lantivet Bay. Passing one derelict lookout and another completely wrecked, you reach a National Trust sign for Blackbottle Rock and soon there is a preview ahead, not only of the rugged coast to be tackled but as far afield as Rame Head near Plymouth.

On along the cliff edge and down steps, the way winds round the back of Lantic Bay, at the far end of which is a stile (path left to Lanteglos church). Here the coast path drops right and keeps left at the

Looking back across the Fowey Estuary to Gribbin Head (centre)

next fork (right descends further to the beach), out onto Pencarrow Head. As you veer north round the headland, Lansallos hamlet is seen on its hillside ahead, but otherwise the surroundings are wild and unsullied by man.

The curious building below is a derelict watch-house. Beyond a gate/stile, keep ahead over level ground, drop over a stream and continue on undulations along vegetated cliffs above Lantivet Bay. Reaching a field track, keep to the lower of 2 paths, down over a wall stile. Two stiles and a footbridge later, you turn up left and beyond the next stile sharp right uphill between low trees. Go over yet another stile on the right and continue along the cliffs contouring between bracken.

At a National Trust sign there is a path left up West Combe to **LANSALLOS** hamlet *(National Trust car park; telephone; no facilities)*. The coast path now crosses a small footbridge and climbs past a conspicuous white beacon marking the dangerous Udder Rock a mile offshore; its position is also denoted by a bell-buoy. More legwork is needed to regain the 400ft. (122m) contour, though none of these high cliffs is precipitous.

Almost immediately the path dives steeply down and up over a stream valley, after which easier walking for a while leads to a sudden

Polperro

spectacular viewpoint at a rocky outcrop. Another steep and earthy descent - lethal in wet conditions - takes you to a little headland above Shag Rock and here the path gets dangerously close to the unstable edge, demanding great care.

After the next stream valley, rocky steps eventually climb to a more well walked section of path, increasingly enclosed by vegetation and provided with a pleasant shelter and numerous benches - sure signs of impending civilisation! At Chapel Cliff, keep left and enter another example of a fishing village-turned-tourist showpiece - **POLPERRO** *(shops; pubs; eating places; accommodation; art galleries; museum; buses for Looe; summer parking ¾ mile (1,200m) inland; toilets).*

Like Clovelly in North Devon, Polperro's picture-postcard charm is exploited to the full so that during the holiday season it receives a daily influx of sightseers from endless cars and coaches which, also like Clovelly, are parked well away from the village itself. Arriving on foot is certainly advantageous and it is pleasant enough mingling with the crowds and wondering at the narrow streets of white painted dwellings which seem almost tossed together in their steep-sided cleft.

Cross the stream at the back of the harbour inlet and walk seawards along a street, climbing past rows of benches. At a path junction by a National Trust sign for The Warren, fork up left (to Talland Bay), where concrete gives way to a normal cliff path. Contouring easily, you pass a path off left and come to a World War I memorial cross on Downend Point - what a magnificent spot! Descending gently to a lane end, keep ahead until the lane veers left then turn off right through low trees, dropping right again to **TALLAND BAY** *(small seasonal cafe/beach shop; hotel just inland at Porthallow; telephone; car park; toilets).*

By the toilets the coast path turns right along to the lane end, then left - not too clearly - up to the cliff path through undergrowth. Walk ahead over a grassy car park and on along the lane past the Smugglers Rest pub, cafe and car park. Turn right through the small car park and up a path to the left. Meandering along pleasant grassy hillside, you may spot a pair of black and white beacons which, together with another pair on the headland above Looe Island, are used by the Admiralty to measure an exact nautical mile during speed trials.

This delightful path continues round Hore Stone and climbs a flight of steps from the top of which the first buildings of Looe are in sight. Progressing round the back of Portnadler Bay, the way undulates and drops over a stream above its waterfall beach outlet. Beyond a substantial stile the going is flat and grassy, with only a small stream to cross before reaching Marine Drive *(2 cafes)*. Continue along the roadside, past large residences and hotels and when the road drops (no pavement), watch for steps on the right to the quayside which will lead

Talland Bay

you to the main road bridge connecting the west and east portions of **LOOE** *(all shops, services and accommodation; 2 old pubs; museum; Tourist Information; British Rail branch line terminus; buses; boats for hire; shark fishing centre; car parks; toilets; early closing Thursday).* If you do not wish to spend time in the town, take the small summer ferry directly across the harbour.

Two river valleys have combined at Looe to form a broader and deeper inlet than on neighbouring stretches of coast. Before 1832, when West and East Looe were separate communities with their own MP's and churches, they were important trading and fishing ports. The town's excellent harbour dries out at low tide but still supports a small fishing industry, shark fishing being a speciality popular with visitors. Beaches can be found at Hannafore (West Looe) and at East Looe seafront. In clear weather the Eddystone lighthouse is visible, 11 miles (18km) out to sea. The double-sided town offers a range of interest and amenity for the visitor and there is the added attraction of boating and quayside activity within the harbour itself.

SECTION 9 - Looe to Plymouth;   19 miles (31km)

A long day which could be split. Short cuts are possible near the end and most of the walking is fairly undemanding. Residential settlements lead first to the beach and holiday village of Millendreath where the clifftops are regained on a more recently opened stretch of path through luxuriant woods to the small resort of Seaton. Beach walking to Downderry is followed by high, vegetated clifftops and a poorly defined section over rough pasture to tiny Portwrinkle, where there is a beach alternative if tide and firing ranges allow. Skirting a golf course, then circumventing the M.O.D.'s Tregantle Fort, the coast path returns to the roadside above sands and stays on it past holiday chalets at Freathy. If not short-cutting Rame Head, you take the path to Polhawn Cove and reach the headland itself with wide sea views. Pleasant going above Plymouth Sound leads to the twin fishing villages of Cawsand and Kingsand and a mixed terrain walk through a country park to Cremyll and the Plymouth ferry.   Grading - moderate.

Shops, pubs and eating places at Millendreath. Shop, pub, beach cafe and accommodation at Seaton. Shops, pub, refreshments and accommodation at Downderry. Pub and accommodation off-route at Crafthole. General store at Freathy. Seasonal cafe and roadside restaurants above Tregonhawke Beach. Shops, services and accommodation at Cawsand and Kingsand, also ferry direct to Plymouth. Pub, seasonal refreshments and some accommodation at Cremyll.

The coast path routing leaves East Looe left up Castle Street (by

West Looe from East Looe

Dewhursts butchers shop on Fore Street), goes over a little crossroads and on up along the broad East Cliff Walk which soon becomes a path above the beach. Emerging at narrow Plaidy Lane, turn down right past the Bodrigy cafe and beach. Continue forward past secluded properties at Plaidy and just after the lane begins to rise, watch for the coast path up right beneath trees, leading out to a residential cul-de-sac. Where the roadway bends left, keep ahead between 2 houses (waymarked) and down steps to **MILLENDREATH BEACH** (*supermarket; Tinners Arms and Davy's Locker pubs; restaurant; Valley Club; amusements; telephone; boats for hire; tennis; crazy golf etc; toilets.*)

This colony of holiday chalets and caravans appears rather brash but its holidaymakers are well provided for and the modest sandy beach is safe for children. Walk straight along the seafront and up the road past an 'Unstable Cliffs - Keep Clear' notice. The road climbs past houses, becomes a track overhung with trees and narrows to a path gaining height to Bodigga clifftops and a good viewpoint.

Proceed ahead along the tarred lane near Bodigga Farm for about 300m and turn off right at a stile and coast path sign by a large tree - the start of a fairly recent section of path. As you go round by a fence, there are superb views back to Looe and its island. Drop to a sign and turn left along the cliffs, the way now undulating along partly wooded and bracken-covered slopes.

Before long you descend through deep woods *(path off left to Mur-rraytown Monkey Sanctuary, an unusual zoo housing a collection of Brazilian woolly monkeys)*. The coast path drops and climbs through the trees which are densely overgrown with luxuriant vegetation in summer, and eventually becomes more open again along brackeny slopes. It veers

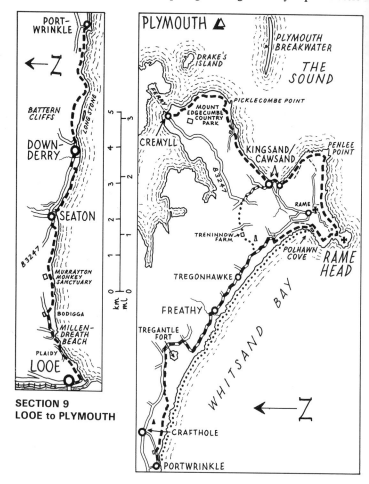

**SECTION 9
LOOE to PLYMOUTH**

The beach between Seaton and Downderry

inland and ends in steps to the road, down which turn right to
SEATON *(shop; pub; beach cafes; caravan park; some accommodation; telephone; buses for Looe and Plymouth; car park; toilets; early closing Thursday).* Seaton's large beach of coarse grey-brown sand is sombre in even the brightest weather!

Cross the stream and walk either along the beach (the best way) or on the B3247 coast road, depending on the tide. Cliffs hereabouts are extremely unstable, threatening properties built on them - witness the concrete sea defences, intact or otherwise, and several warning notices. If you take the beach route, you will be crossing bands of red rock and grey boulders, though farther along the sand reverts to a more normal hue. Pass a path up left and a slipway *(access here to campsite 500m inland: go up to the main road, turn right and look for sign on the left).*

In less than 2 miles (3km) from Seaton the route comes up to **DOWNDERRY** *(shops, refreshments; Ship Inn; accommodation; telephone; car park)* and turns right along the coast road as far as the left hairpin. Here turn off right, just before the entrance to Downderry Lodge.

The path twists up to the top of Battern Cliffs, at 461ft. (141m) the highest in south Cornwall. Cross a stile and turn down right round a field edge, high above the jagged Long Stone offshore. Having passed

93

through a gate and turned right, there are informative views over the countryside inland and forward to Rame Head, a major promontory protecting Plymouth Sound from the south-west, and the day's main objective.

There was no waymarking here at the author's last visit, but you keep outside the field fence - there may be small diversions back to the cliff edge due to electric fencing. Climb to a stile in a field corner and continue ahead over sheep pasture, possibly over another electric fence: the path is poorly defined. Cross a wire fence below a black and white pole marker and pass another close by the path before crossing the stile seawards of a bungalow.

Walking on along grassy cliffsides, you soon drop round a field perimeter to a gate leading out to a narrow lane. Turn right to the little seafront at **PORTWRINKLE** *(licensed hotel uphill at Crafthole; telephone; car parking; toilets)*. There is a diminutive sand and shingle beach and a rocky foreshore.

Stay on the seafront road past houses, 2 parking areas and the toilets, ignorning a footpath right to the beach and continuing instead up the road towards Whitsand Bay Golf Clubhouse, opposite which turn right *(accommodation up road at Crafthole)*. NOTE: In certain circumstances it is feasible to walk right along the sands of Whitsand Bay from Portwrinkle to Polhawn Cove near Rame Head. However, this depends on no firing being in progress and on favourable tides. A word of warning: the tide does come in very quickly and there are dangerous currents. A few escape paths lead up to the road. Also the last mile is awkward and rocky but if conditions are right, the beach is certainly an enjoyable alternative.

You now climb up to a golf tee and walk along the golf course's seaward edge, in a few hundred metres forking right. Follow a field edge right, to a signpost, then veer left, passing 2 more black and white poles and M.O.D. 'Danger - Keep Out' notices. **TREGANTLE FORT** is a military training camp and it is quite likely you will hear firing on the ranges and encounter crocodiles of recruits on training marches in the vicinity. Live firing is in progress when red flags are flying or lamps are displayed.

Cross a field wall stile and follow the perimeter to the road at a National Trust 'Trethill Cliffs' sign. Here you turn sharp right immediately, over a stone stile and along a confined corridor of land between road-hedge and M.O.D. fence - monotonous but much better than taking to the road!

Topping a rise, you gain your first tentative views of urban Plymouth beyond a skyline of fields and trees. Keep straight on, crossing

Tregantle Fort

a couple of tracks, to the road junction to Torpoint where the coast path drops to the verge and eventually onto the road itself. From a lay-by are comprehensive views over Plymouth city.

Keep on the road past Tregantle Fort entrance and turn right at a sign for Whitsand Bay, Freathy Cliff and Tregonhawke Cliff *(campsite at Tregonhawke)*. Tregantle Fort appears as a massive, sprawling grey building surrounded by firing ranges and warning notices.

It is possible to walk on the verge of the coast road for some distance and when you have passed a car park above Sharrow Point, there is a small general store up left at **FREATHY** should you need provisions. The road winds past numerous chalets and bungalows perched on terraces on the high, rambling cliffs with marvellous sea views. The monument is in memory of a young man drowned on Whitsand Beach, underlining its dangers. 200m beyond Whitsand Bay car park *(seasonal Cliff Top cafe 50m down to the right; Eddystone Cafe and toilets farther down on Tregonhawke Beach)* stand the Rame Head and Cabin restaurants. If time presses or a circumvention of Rame Head is to be missed out for any reason, fork left (north-east) here on a waymarked path past an air-navigation beacon to Treninnow Farm (½ mile) and a quiet lane to a crossroads where a right turn will lead down to Kingsand. This saves about 3½ miles (6km) distance.

The coast path turns right opposite a small car park in a road

St.Michael's Chapel on Rame Head

junction, signed 'Rame Head 1¾ miles', and forks left immediately by a 'Beware dangerous cliff path' sign. You then swing back south-east and descend gently, passing Plymouth Y.M.C.A.'s 'Wiggle Hut' - a stone lean-to - before emerging behind a row of white cottages where you fork left. Go through the gate, up steps, over a track, up more steps, over a stile and out onto open hillside above a chalet and a former military fortification at Polhawn Cove. It is worth pausing here to look back at the long arc of Whitsand Bay.

Aim for a stile in hedges, after which the narrow path snakes out past a bench viewpoint at a rocky rise, revealing Rame Head with its chapel ruin rising dramatically ahead. Soon the path lies over turf, past a lookout post to a waymark signpost. Turn right towards the chapel, or double back left through gorse.

If conditions are good, the short detour out onto the headland is recommended for views back to Dodman Point and out to the Eddy-stone lighthouse 9 miles (14km) offshore. Guarding the western entrance to Plymouth Sound, **RAME HEAD** rears 300ft. (91m) above the sea. The ruinous chapel perched on the summit was dedicated to St. Michael in 1397.

On a good wide path past the Coastguard station leading easily along clifftops above Plymouth Sound, you pass a path left to Rame church (15th century and still candle-lit) and another to a car park just before Penlee Point. From this turning point, keep right, down a metalled

Cawsand

lane past a foghorn (which can start anytime without warning!). Entering shady woods, watch for the coast path forking down right. Go forward on the metalled lane and in 100m fork right again on a level pathway. At a road turning area by cottages, keep straight ahead along the pathway to the small fishing village of **CAWSAND** *(food shop; pubs; restaurant; beach cafe; accommodation; toilets; boats for hire; buses for Plymouth; summer ferry to Plymouth's Mayflower Steps, weather permitting every 1½ hours).*

It is but a few minutes stroll past guest-houses to the clock tower at **KINGSAND** *(shops; pubs; cafe; restaurant; accommodation; car park; toilets; buses for Plymouth)*, a slightly larger twin to Cawsand and with a similar small shingly beach. Cawsand has roots back in the Middle Ages and during the 18th century was an active smuggling port thanks to its shoreline caves. There remains an authenticity about these little fishing villages which have avoided the commercialisation of so many other places in the south-west.

Go up Kingsand's main street past the clock tower and turn up Market Street past the Rising Sun pub then into Lower Row. Go through the gate into Mount Edgecumbe Country Park (signed to Hooe Lake), now on a broad path along gentle slopes and through a copse.

Offshore, **PLYMOUTH BREAKWATER** can be seen end-on, a

vital protection even today for shipping entering and leaving port. So many ships were lost prior to 1788 that a scheme was voiced to construct a huge breakwater and so provide the British fleet with a well protected anchorage. Nothing was done, however, during the French revolutionary wars and it was not until 1806 that the project was revived and plans drawn up by the celebrated Scots engineer John Rennie.

Again the scheme was shelved and more ships lost. So urgent had the situation become that in 1812 the first huge foundation block was dropped and although gales often set the work back and wrecks continued to occur, the breakwater was finally completed in 1841. It had taken 4½ million tons of limestone and granite to form the mile-long structure which encloses 5 square miles of open water 2 miles out from the Hoe foreshore. The cost was £1½ million and the lives of many seamen during the long delays in adopting the plan and its final realisation.

The onward coast path contours above bracken and gorse on low cliffs and, just past a white marker beacon on the right, reaches the road opposite a large house. Turn right, then in 50m go left over a stile on a path parallel to the road and slanting up to a gate into oak woods. The level way now winds round past mossy walls and rhododendrons, through a decripit archway then zig-zags down right through the trees to a pebbly beach at Picklecombe Point. Almost immediately you veer up left and soon descend by a white temple folly, a lake and picnic tables in **MOUNT EDGECUMBE COUNTRY PARK,** overlooking ships in the Sound and Drake's Island.

Walk along the concrete track, across more lawns and through a gate into formal gardens. A spacious cafe *(meals, snacks, drinks)* leads on to the entrance to Mount Edgecumbe mansion, rebuilt after bombing in 1941; owned jointly by Cornwall and Plymouth, its grounds are open all year, the house on summer Monday and Tuesday afternoons.

This is **CREMYLL** *(pub; refreshment kiosk)* and a frequent ferry (whose history dates back some 600 years) runs seven days a week to Plymouth - ½-hourly in summer, hourly in winter; tickets at turnstile. You sail past the Mayflower International Marina with its complement of unguessably expensive yachts and from the landing slipway in Devon, walk up Admirals Hard (or catch a bus to the city centre). Walkers follow signs for the Ferry Port and go round the back of Stonehouse Docks basin. Turn right for the Hoe, from where it is not far to the centre of **PLYMOUTH** *(all shops, services and accommodation; youth hostel; Tourist Information; British Rail main line station;*

Plymouth Hoe

coach and bus station; etc.).

Situated at the mouth of the rivers Tamar and Plym and their tributaries, this famous natural anchorage became established as a naval port during the Middle Ages and the French revolutionary wars. The city is inextricably linked with Sir Francis Drake and the Spanish Armada, with the historic voyage of the 'Mayflower' in 1620 and, in more recent times, with ocean racing, from Tall Ships to single-handed craft. Devonport Docks remain important, despite the numerical reduction in Britain's naval fleet, while the commercial port handles industrial and passenger-ferry trade.

Plymouth city centre was virtually levelled by air-raids in 1941 and has been completely rebuilt. The well known Hoe, with its promenade, monuments, old lighthouse and views of shipping, is well worth seeing, as are 16th century houses in New Street near Sutton Harbour and the old Barbican - all within a compact area on the site of the original old town.

CHAPTER 2

Plymouth to Exmouth
(89 miles - 143km)

From coastal fortifications overlooking the Sound, small resorts popular with Plymouth's inhabitants lead to a summer ferry over the River Yealm and the sailing centre of Newton Ferrers. An old carriage drive is followed for several miles before the cliff path reaches the beautiful River Erme's mouth, which must be waded or an inland detour made.

Strenuous gradients bring you to Bigbury-on-Sea and Burgh Island where a seasonal ferry crosses the River Avon estuary. Easy going on popular coastline to the fishing village of Hope gives way to Bolt Tail headland and magnificent clifftop walking along Heritage Coast over Bolt Head to the yachting town of Salcombe. Initially wild and unfrequented, the coast path crosses dramatic Start Point, passes the sad ruins of Hallsands and descends to Torcross for a shingle trudge between the sea and Slapton Ley Nature Reserve along to Strete Gate, where the road is taken to Stoke Fleming.

Plenty of ups and downs lie along the lonely cliffs between Dartmouth and the limestone of Berry Head above Brixham's busy harbour. Before long the coast path as such disappears on the built-up seafront round Torbay. Promenade, gardens and open spaces at Torquay are followed by woods and downland to Babbacombe and varied terrain from the cliff railway through woodland and along a cliffside ledge to Maidencombe.

Harder going through steep combes is alleviated beyond Teignmouth by progress on beach, sea wall or road parallel to the railway line through Dawlish. A short stretch of road from Dawlish Warren to Starcross takes you to a year-round ferry over the River Exe and hence to Exmouth.

SECTION 10 - Plymouth to Newton Ferrers/Noss Mayo; 8 miles (13km)

An interesting section, despite its proximity to Plymouth city. From Turnchapel, a road past coastal fortifications and with good views of the Sound

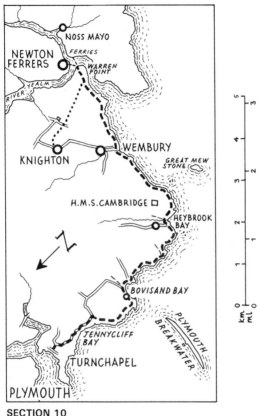

SECTION 10
PLYMOUTH to NEWTON FERRERS/ NOSS MAYO

is followed by sometimes overgrown cliffs and a descent to Bovisand Bay, first of many small holiday resorts in South Devon. Low cliffs lead on to Heybrook Bay and a close encounter with a Royal Naval gunnery school. The larger village of Wembury (optional return to Plymouth by bus) stands little more than a mile from a ferry over the River Yealm estuary to Newton Ferrers or Noss Mayo.

Refreshments at Jennycliff Bay; refreshments at Bovisand Bay - both seasonal. Pub, limited accommodation at Heybrook Bay. Shops, refreshments and limited accommodation at Wembury.

NOTE: For long-distance walkers, reaching Plymouth and the Cornwall/Devon border is a major milestone; it can also act well as a starting or finishing point for a coastal walk of several days' duration (in either direction) as communications with the rest of the country are so good. However, as often happens when the South West Way enters a conurbation, finding the way out can cause problems!

As if this were not enough, the onward route is further complicated by having to cross 3 river estuaries in quick succession - 2 with infrequent summer-only ferries and 1 with no ferry at all! Should river levels be high due to tide, gales or heavy rain, or should you be walking out of season, the author's advice is to catch a bus from Plymouth to Kingsbridge and a further bus or taxi to Bantham on the east bank of the third estuary, the River Avon. (In fact, the first section of path from Turnchapel to Warren Point can be walked separately, with a bus ride back to the city.)

Lest this paints too gloomy a picture of the walking ahead, it should be said that the coastal scenery is marvellously unspoiled for much of the way and the River Erme estuary is reputed to be one of the country's loveliest. Provided you are planning to walk during the main summer season and you don't mind the occasional wait for ferry or tide, there is no reason to be discouraged.

The South Devon coast path starts at **TURNCHAPEL.** The ferry has, unfortunately, long since disappeared but a bus can be taken to avoid excessive street bashing. From above the waterfront, walk south-west along the road past Stamford Fort, now a holiday centre, reaching open slopes above Jennycliff Bay *(seasonal refreshments; summertime buses for Plymouth; car park; toilets; excellent views across the Sound).* Where the road veers inland just before a little valley, turn off right onto the cliff path. This is not always cleared on Staddon Heights but eventually improves, with a close-up, end-on view of the great breakwater only a few hundred metres away.

A footbridge over an old ropeway channel then steps lead down to converted Coastguard cottages at Bovisand harbour, built in the early 1800's as a water supply point for ships. Bovisand Fort is a well preserved example of 19th century Palmerston fortifications (later dubbed 'follies' as they were never needed) - part of Plymouth's defence against the French naval threat. Today the Fort is a training base for marine activities and water sports.

Once beyond Bovisand Bay *(refreshments; telephone; car parking; toilets; buses for Plymouth)* with its caravans and chalets, the way proceeds along cliffs above Andurn Point to the seaward end of Heybrook Bay *(pub; some accommodation; telephone; buses for Plymouth;*

car parking). Continuing south-east, ignore the clear uphill track, turning off right instead after the last house.

HMS CAMBRIDGE is a Royal Navy gunnery school and notices warn you to expect noise from firing (the guns are quite close!). During firing practice, the coast path through this Danger Area is closed (usually weekdays) and red flags are displayed. At such times, a waymarked diversion will take you through the grounds of the establishment.

Generating considerbly fewer decibels than the gunnery range, gulls might draw your attention to the Great Mew Stone offshore, a breeding spot of kittiwakes, fulmars and other seabirds, as well as rats! Unbelievably, a succession of people have lived on the Stone's southern side, but the rock is now owned by the M.O.D.

Along the edge of low cliffs, the coast path arrives at **WEMBURY** and adjacent **KNIGHTON** *(shops; refreshments; limited accommodation; Post Office; telephone; National Trust Centre; buses for Plymouth; car park; toilets).* Above Wembury's interesting sandy beach stands the prominent tower of its 15th century church, a useful landmark from the sea.

Pastureland through National Trust property leads you towards the wooded mouth of the River Yealm (pronounced 'Yam'). You pass the erstwhile Coastguard Rocket House and drop steeply to shoreline steps at **WARREN POINT.** By shouting 'Ferry'! you will procure passage across the Yealm - during July and August only, as things stand at present. The ferry operates between 11.00am. and 1.00pm; 2.30pm and 4.00pm. (earlier and later in good weather). For confirmation telephone (0752) 872189.

You thus reach either the sailing centre of **NEWTON FERRERS** *(shops, services and accommodation; pubs; campsite; telephone; buses for Plymouth),* then walking east to cross an arm of the estuary at Bridgend before returning west to Noss Mayo...or you ferry directly across to **NOSS MAYO** *(pubs),* a charming backwater hamlet of medieval origins.

NOTE: From here to Bigbury-on-Sea - a distance of some 14 miles (23km) - there are no on-route refreshment or accommodation points except a seasonal shop/cafe at Stoke House and refreshments at Mothecombe. It is therefore prudent to stock up with the necessary provisions, particularly as the River Erme has to be crossed: with no ferry, this can mean waiting for the tide or making a lengthy inland detour.

Should the ferry over the Yealm not be running, it may be feasible to catch a bus for Newton Ferrers or Noss Mayo from Plymouth. In this case, return to the Rocket House where a large gate leads to a track through a field, becoming a road. From Wembury House, a stile and subsequent fields lead over to Knighton and buses for Plymouth.

SECTION 11 - Newton Ferrers/Noss Mayo to Bigbury-on-Sea; 13 miles (21km)

A walk whose flow can be interrupted by having to wade the River Erme - details below. Otherwise a varied and entertaining stretch of largely unspoiled coast, starting with several miles on an old carriage drive and an optional detour to view a restored 14th century chapel. Leaving the carriage drive, cliff path undulations lead past a dramatic rock outcrop and a pleasant cove near the Erme's tranquil estuary mouth. At low water you wade the river at an old road ford and resume cliff edge walking outside fields. The going becomes much more strenuous thereafter, with 3 big combes to negotiate and care is needed on steep slopes either side of the coves. You soon reach the holiday settlements of Challaborough and Bigbury-on-Sea. Burgh Island, in view for much of this walk, makes an interesting diversion on foot or by 'sea-tractor'. Grading - Easy to Beacon Hill then more difficult. Strenuous in places between Erme Mouth and Challaborough.

Possible shop/summer refreshments at Stoke House. Summer refreshments at Mothecombe.

NOTE: Before leaving Noss Mayo, do ensure you have tide times for the River Erme estuary (tide tables are widely available from bookshops/newsagents, while tide times for the Erme and Avon rivers are quoted in the South West Way Association's annual handbook). Arriving outside the 'wading window' of 1 hour each side of low water can entail a very long wait, with a highly undesirable alternative of diverting inland as far as Sequers Bridge on the A379 - an additional distance of some 9 miles (14km). Even if you are on target for the tide, an onshore gale or a river swollen by recent rain will frustrate your crossing.

Beyond the Erme there are some fierce ups and downs to contend with, so carry sufficient energy food as the refreshment points mentioned in the text are not 100% reliable and in any case are high-summer season only.

The road west from Noss Mayo becomes a wide track soon after the ferry slipway and former Coastguard cottages. This easily graded carriage drive was made in the late 1800's at the instigation of Lord Revelstoke, whose estate it encircled and along which he would impress distinguished guests with views of his land holdings and the

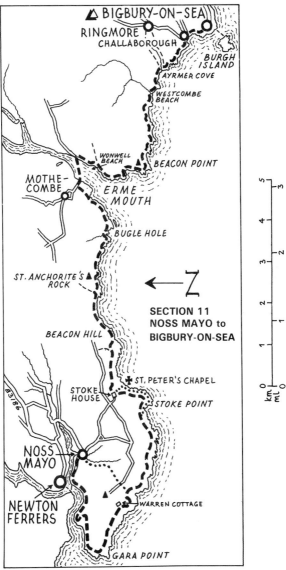

SECTION 11
NOSS MAYO to
BIGBURY-ON-SEA

coastal scenery. Resembling the 'Hobby Drive' near Clovelly on Devon's north coast, this private driveway is followed by the coast path for about 5 miles (8km), though its surface has of course deteriorated through neglect and the passage of time.

Rising gently and turning south-west, 200ft. (61m) above Gara Point, there are superb views back along the Cornish coast in good weather. 500m beyond Warren Cottages you pass an access track left to a car park: if quick progress from Noss Mayo is of the essence, take the track south from the village, up the stream valley and join the coast path here.

The surrounding countryside appears surprisingly remote and remains unspoiled mainly due to its inaccessibility by major roads, which are forced well inland to cross river valleys. This area of south Devon between Dartmoor and the sea and bordered by the Yealm and Dart rivers is known as South Hams.

Past Stoke Point, the track enters woods and comes inland a little to a road junction at the small settlement of **STOKE HOUSE** *(possible summer shop/refreshments; telephone; car parking).* Just before rounding Stoke Point, it is possible to branch down right by a caravan park and come round to the partly restored 14th century St. Peter's Chapel, once the parish church of Noss Mayo. This diversion is completed by walking up a steep holiday camp road to Stoke House.

The overgrown carriage drive continues for another ¾ mile (1,200m) before swinging inland at the site of ruined Membland tea house on **BEACON HILL.** Here the coast path forks right downhill and the going is immediately more characteristic of a cliff path, with some legwork to do to pass an old quarry and reach St. Anchorite's Rock, a large outcrop whose summit is an easy scramble. (Ignore the track inland to Carswell just before rising to the rock.)

Hugging the rugged cliffs for about 1km, the field edge path takes you down a steep drop to Battisborough stream at Bugle Hole, a pleasant spot in which to while away time if waiting for the tide to fall. A recently opened section of path now passes through a gate, staying on the coast as a clear track round **ERME MOUTH,** through trees and past a slipway to Mothecombe. Here the country road ends in a ford across the river, and just up left in a field behind the old village school is a car park with summer refreshments.

Belonging to the Flete Estate, Mothecombe and the Erme estuary have undergone virtually no modern development. In consequence, the area is the very picture of tranquility - rare on Devon's popular south coast.

In normal conditions it is possible to wade the Erme from the row of

Coastguard cottages along the line of the old ford (east-north-east), one hour each side of low water, although as already pointed out this can be dangerous after heavy rain or in high seas. At the far side you join the road end from Kingston to Wonwell Beach. In very dry conditions it may be possible to wade directly across to Wonwell beach cove (south-east) but care should be exercised owing to the uneven river bed.

Once safely across the estuary to the road end, walk into the woods and take the obvious path right (south-west) to Wonwell Beach, with its one-time Pilot House and old limekiln. Walk across the top of the beach and on along clifftop field edges, climbing gently past a marvellous rocky viewpoint near Fernycombe Beach and up to Beacon Point, 308ft. (94m) above the sea at the western end of Bigbury Bay.

The next few miles are surprisingly strenuous after mostly easy going so far. 3 big combes lie ahead and their fierce gradients demand surefootedness as well as adequate energy reserves, especially in rough weather. The section is not a long one, however, and as you approach Burgh Island, the small resort of Bigbury-on-Sea is near at hand.

Throughout the remainder of the walk, the coast path is hemmed in between an unwelcome barbed wire field fence and the cliff edge, at times perilously close to the latter! The first combe is the hardest to negotiate as you drop very steeply from Hoist Point to Westcombe Beach. The following up-and-down is through Ayrmer Cove with its great shining faces of Dartmouth slate. *(Paths up left lead to Ringmore - about a mile - a delightful little village with a pub, some accommodation and an interesting 13th century church.)*

Over the next hill lies the holiday settlement of **CHALLABOR-OUGH** *(pub, cafe and beach shop attached to a caravan park; telephone).* Dangerous currents detract from bathing here, though a summer lifeguard is in attendance. You now pass behind the beach, crossing the stream and in 500m arrive at **BIGBURY-ON-SEA** *(shops, services and accommodation; youth hostel; Post Office; summer buses for Plymouth; car park; toilets; access to Burgh Island; early closing Thursday).*

Bigbury has a long stretch of moderately shelving sand but bathing can be hazardous in the river mouth area. This bungalow resort enjoys a unique position and can get very crowded in summer. A major attraction is Burgh Island, whose profile is somewhat marred by obtrusive building but which is itself well worth a visit. You can walk the 300m over the sands at low tide; in deeper water, the island hotel's sea-tractor serves as a ferry along the causeway and is specially designed with long legs to operate in up to 3m depth and in rough seas. The island's 14th century Pilchard Inn stands adjacent to a former millionaire's home, now an hotel. A ruined 'huer's hut' - where pilchard shoals were once spotted - tops the high ground and is a fine spot for views of seabirds and the coastline.

SECTION 12 - Bigbury-on-Sea to Salcombe;   13 miles (21km)

Another river estuary presents possible crossing problems but is followed by straightforward walking along low cliffs by a golf course in the popular holiday area around Thurlestone and South Milton Sands. A short walk ensues over to the twin fishing villages of Outer and Inner Hope and an ascent to Bolt Tail. From this major headland, National Trust Heritage Coast leads along high, open clifftops, over a deep combe in rocky terrain and out to Bolt Head. The way reaches Salcombe by path or an old paved track to the estuary road.   Grading - moderate but more difficult in places from Hope Cove to Salcombe.

Pubs and accommodation in Bantham. Hotel and some accommodation off-route at Thurlestone. Refreshments and accommodation at South Milton Sands. Shops, refreshments and accommodation at Outer/Inner Hope. Meals, drinks and accommodation at Port Light Hotel/Restaurant.

The third of the troublesome trio of river estuaries now has to be crossed. Although several major rivers still lie ahead along the south coast, they are all provided with regular, year-round ferries and present coastal walkers with no problems.

Leave Bigbury-on-Sea by turning right at the bottom of the B3392 road (to Bigbury) onto a small hill at the mouth of the River Avon. This little stretch of path was the first suggested improvement by the South West Way Association to become officially integrated into the long-distance route. It postpones road walking, but there are still a few hundred metres on busy tarmac to Mount Folly Farm, though estuary views are excellent. Turn right alongside the farm buildings and drop to riverbank sands at Cockleridge, opposite the Bantham ferry point. (At low tide you can walk along the sands from Bigbury but you will miss the wide views.)

The ferry runs for 2 weeks over Easter then from Whitsun to the end of August: Monday to Saturday 10.00am. to 11.00am. and 3.00pm. to 4.00pm. Clearly this is a very restricted service and once again walkers face a long inland detour to the A379 road bridge at Aveton Gifford if the ferry is not operating. The alternative strategy is a wading attempt.

NOTE: Wading the Avon is more hazardous than the Erme and should only be attempted in perfect conditions, ie. low river level, low tide and calm sea. The author has no first-hand experience of this, but

Bantham Beach and Burgh Island (centre top)

quotes the following advice from the SWWA handbook: Leave from the well defined hedge running north-to-south with pine trees, and head towards a castellated building with a little flagpole in the middle on the east bank (or vice versa if walking west). It is important not to wade across elsewhere despite tempting shallows, as there are unexpected deeper channels of soft sand. Nearer to the sea are dangerous tidal currents. In any event, expect to get wet - at least to thigh depth!

From the ferry slipway, walk up to the road and turn right along it to a large car park *(toilets)* in sandhills known as the Ham. *(A short distance along the road to the left, however, are 2 good pubs offering accommodation and a restaurant in Bantham village.)* All along the head of the popular sandy shore at the River Avon's mouth are large notices warning of dangerous bathing. Nevertheless, there are safer parts which are also signed, and a summer lifeguard is in attendance.

Proceed to the bottom left-hand corner of the car park (or walk right round the protruding spit of land to the north-west) and along a sandy track past Bantham Surf Lifesaving Club. Cross a stile at a cliff subsidence sign and walk on round open clifftop with excellent views of Burgh Island and the sweep of Bantham Beach.

Soon you come alongside Thurlestone Golf Course, keeping to the seaward perimeter until dropping to a small cove and dunes. Here you will see the first of several earnest notices 'Beware of golf balls before

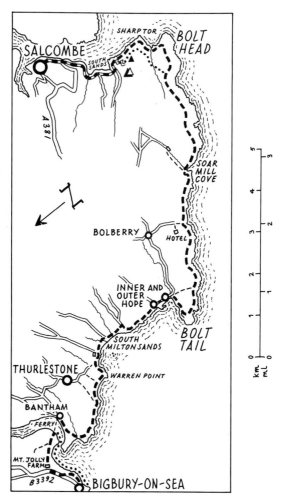

SECTION 12
BIGBURY-ON-SEA to SALCOMBE

proceeding'. Just how you do so without sight of the golfers is not clear! Flippancy apart, there is a report of a walker being hit badly in the face by a golf ball.

Stay seaward and follow the odd waymark arrows. As you come round Warren Point to face a large hotel, notice the arched rock in the bay. In Old English 'Thurlestone' means pierced stone and the old village itself *(hotel; some accommodation; Post Office; telephone; summer buses for Kingsbridge)* is situated about 500m off-route inland from the golf clubhouse.

Walk round the back of the little beach, turn right along the road past extraordinary wind-sculpted trees then go straight ahead between walls and on up a tarmac path past the imposing hotel *(refreshments)*. The cliff edge is crumbling badly here. Go down through a small car park and at a turning area at the bottom of the lane, continue between fences and over a long footbridge spanning South Milton Ley, a Devon Bird-Watching and Preservation Society nature reserve. With binoculars you might spot such species as heron, sedge warblers and moorhens.

Turning seawards, you reach a National Trust car park at **SOUTH MILTON SANDS** *(small beach cafe/ice-creams)*. Walk along the stony track behind the beach and keep left inland behind an hotel ahead *(beach shop/refreshments)*. Pass another hotel *(cream teas this time!)* and where the road swings left, turn right past 'La Mer'. Where this lane veers left, keep ahead back to the clifftop.

At the author's last visit, re-seeding was in progress but small diversions like this are unpredictable. The coast path climbs over Great Ledge Cliff and descends a grassy sward into **OUTER HOPE** *(pub; Post Office/general store; restaurant and cafe; accommodation; telephone; car park; toilets; limited bus service)*. Not far ahead along a tarmac path round Hope Cove lies **INNER HOPE** (and 200m up left off-route its little square of picturesque old Devon cottages). These much photographed twin fishing villages get overrun with visitors in the summer, although walkers arriving early or late in the day probably see them at their best.

The onward route mounts steps by the old lifeboat station (transferred in 1887 to South Sands and later to Salcombe) to a sign for Bolt Head 7 miles, Salcombe 8½ miles (11km and 14km respectively). This stretch represents some of the finest high cliff walking in south Devon - owned by the National Trust, noted for its flora and fauna and designated 'Heritage Coast' all the way from here to Start Point. It is not all easy going: there are 1 or 2 big climbs and little chance of refreshments.

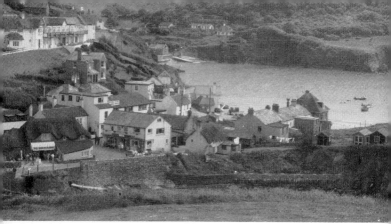

Hope Cove

Sloping up pleasantly past benches, with unimpeachable views past Hope Cove right back to Rame Head, the path approaches **BOLT TAIL** (lower path on the right closed due to erosion). You walk round past the Coastguard lookout and back south-east past the fallen ramparts of south Devon's only Iron Age promontory fort atop this great bastion of sheer rock rising 400ft. (122m) above the sea. In the winter of 1760, 800 people drowned when the 90-gun 'HMS Ramilles' foundered on the fearsome cliffs; the coast between here and Bolt Head is notorious for shipwrecks.

You now meander on through low gorse with marvellous prospects over the rolling Devon countryside of South Hams. Passing a path left to Hope Cove at a gate (a good short circular walk), you continue outside a wire fence past the first of many craggy outcrops. After a stile you are on Bolberry Down and soon come to a National Trust collecting box and a track left to **PORT LIGHT HOTEL** (*meals, drinks, accommodation; campsite at Bolberry*).

Aiming for the radio masts, the coast path dips through a hollow to emerge in a car park by a waymark post. Keep to the seaward path along a well walked crest of land with more interesting outcrops over to the left. The ridge drops spectacularly towards **SOAR MILL COVE** (*hotel 500m up left - east-north-east - and camping ¾ mile, 1,200m*), a deep combe reminiscent of Devon's north coast. The steep descent concludes down steps to the left.

Swinging right alongside the stream to the cove, you go ahead to a signpost (Bolt Head 2 miles) where the path angles across to the bottom of an old wall then climbs determinedly past rock outcrops of mica-schist and quartz up the rugged cliffside. Beyond a stile, aim for

112

Unspoiled 'Heritage Coast' from Bolt Tail to Salcombe

a plank bridge and waymark post, after which the route ascends quite steeply to a conspicuous rocky tor. Veer left in front of it, where a broad turfy track takes you along The Warren above dramatic cliff scenery.

Nearing **BOLT HEAD**, the coast further afield is revealed, including Prawle Point, Devon's most southerly promontory. Go through a wall gap and keep right, over a stile and along a clear path to the headland. (An alternative path to Sharpitor Gardens near Salcombe angles down north-east from above Off Cove, crosses the stream in the valley behind Starehole Bay by a confusing signpost, then climbs rocky steps to a viewing table on Sharp Tor. Pass the triangulation pillar, cross a stile and drop to a sign, turning right to emerge by palm trees at the youth hostel entrance. Turn down left, zig-zagging to the coast road at South Sands.)

The main coast path changes direction abruptly on Bolt Head but stays on the cliff edge to drop over the stream mouth in Starehole Bay. Passing narrowly below Sharp Tor, it continues as the Courtenay Walk, a paved track cut in the last century by the Earl of Devon's son. After a wooded section, it emerges at the road adjacent to Sharpitor Gardens (turn left for the gardens and museum - open daily 11.00am. to 1.00pm., 2.00pm. to 6.00pm., April to October. Overbecks youth hostel is nearby).

Turn right, down to the little estuary-side road at South Sands, an exclusive collection of hotels, and follow the undulations along to

The Salcombe Estuary from Sharp Tor

SALCOMBE *(all shops, services and accommodation; youth hostel; Tourist Information; car parks; toilets; buses for Kingsbridge; ferries and boat trips; early closing Thursday).* One of Britain's most important yachting centres, Salcombe is situated on an estuary with many branches, and in a sheltered spot on Devon's most southerly shore. The climate is mild all year but despite all these favourable factors, the town's potential as a port was always restricted by the existence of sandbanks at the river mouth called The Bar. Fort Charles, off North Sands Beach, was built by Henry VIII and withstood a long seige by the Roundheads during the Civil War. Devoted almost exclusively to the requirements of its boat-owning patrons, Salcombe is an attractive place though not one attuned to the long-distance hiker!

SECTION 13 - Salcombe to Stoke Fleming;   16 miles (26km)

A long day, but becoming progressively easier. Once out of the Salcombe estuary, a rugged path follows wild and unfrequented coastline with no amenities round Prawle Point, Devon's southernmost tip, and past the occasional isolated beach to Start Point, a dramatic headland with a lighthouse. Walking north, you descend to the fascinating ruins of Hallsands village, destroyed by the sea earlier this century. Undulating low cliffs lead on to Torcross, at the southern end of a huge inland lake nature reserve and from where a long, straight trudge between coast road and shingle beach leads to Strete Gate. With no onward coast path available,

114

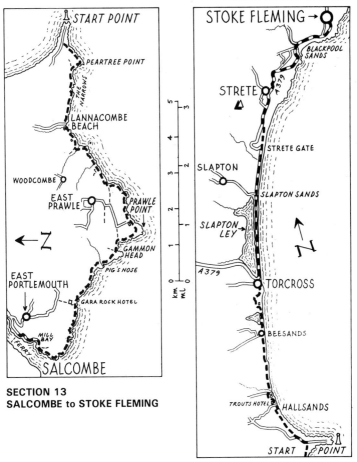

SECTION 13
SALCOMBE to STOKE FLEMING

you take to the road through Strete village, past a popular sandy bay and up to Stoke Fleming. Grading - more difficult to Start Point. Moderate to Torcross. Easy to Stoke Fleming.

Seasonal refreshments at Hallsands and Greenstraight Beach. Pubs, cafe at Beesands. Pubs, restaurants, cafes, shop and accommodation at Torcross. Shop, pub, accommodation and youth hostel at Strete. Seasonal refreshment at Blackpool Bay.

The river crossing to East Portlemouth is easily achieved by ferry, which leaves Salcombe from the bottom of steps at the side of the Midland Bank in Fore Street: November to March - 8.00am. to 5.00pm. hourly. April to October - continuous service until 7.30pm. July and August weekends, also Bank Holidays - 8.30am. start.

NOTE: The first half of this walk is surprisingly remote from human habitation and there are no on-route refreshments or accommodation throughout the rugged 10 miles (16km) round Prawle and Start points to the hamlet of Hallsands - and no real choice until Torcross. Walkers are advised, therefore, to carry adequate food and drink and to be prepared for rough underfoot conditions in places. That said, it is a very fine stretch of coast indeed, gloriously free of holiday crowds whatever the season.

Disembarking from the ferry in East Portlemouth, climb the steps and turn right along the road towards sandy Mill Bay *(small National Trust car park; toilets)*. Once round the back of the bay, turn right (signed Gara Rock), climbing through trees and forking right on the lower path (the left fork climbs then levels off but can be overgrown). There are glimpses of the estuary and sandy coves as you gradually swing south-east below Rickham Common on open, low cliffs.

Between here and Sharp Tor across the estuary, lies The Bar sandbank, a serious hazard to shipping in a southerly gale and scene of Devon's worst lifeboat tragedy when, in 1916, 13 crewmen were drowned after their boat capsized. Also visible to the south-east will be Gammon Head and some impressive cliff scenery frequented by seabirds.

Turning a path corner, you see the thatched white lookout of Gara Rock Hotel, converted from Coastguard cottages. Outcrops of hornblende and mica-schists characterise the cliffsides right along to Hallsands. Keep right at a waymark, down through bracken and soon you join the broad path from the hotel at little Seacombe Sand. Cross the stream footbridge and continue straightforwardly round Deckler's Cliff, the path twisting and undulating before climbing round the back of Pig's Nose.

Over a stream and round a corner, **GAMMON HEAD** is approached through gorse, heather and bracken. Recently acquired by the National Trust, its thrusting profile typifies the rugged grandeur of this coastal section. You drop steeply over rock-slab steps (a prodigious construction feat!), pass a National Trust sign *(path up left to East Prawle - pub, telephone -1¼ miles, 2km)*, keeping to seaward at a waymark post (not up left as suggested). Facing south, these sunny banks support large populations of butterflies, other insects and wild

Ancient wave-cut platforms beyond Prawle Point

plants.

Walking on along rocky hillside and over a wall stile, you are heading for the Coastguard station on **PRAWLE POINT,** Devon's most southerly headland and a good spot for bird-watching, especially during the autumn migrations. Over the stile just before, keep left parallel to a wall and you will reach a marvellous view ahead of wave-cut platforms, or raised beaches. These were formed by wave action when sea levels were higher than today's. The original cliff line, up to 300ft. (90m) high, is now a field-width from the shore and the cultivated land is situated on weathered material slumped down from the higher ground.

You now pass a row of Coastguard cottages to a stile (bridleway left to East Prawle, 1¼ miles (2km); coast path 2 miles (3km) to Lanna-combe). The way keeps to the seaward edge of the field shelf round Langerstone Point with a good view back to Prawle Point's natural arch. Minor cliff falls could occur hereabouts at any time - beware of the crumbling edge.

Coming round a field, you meet a wider path and turn left inland; in 50m turn back right into the next field on the other side of the wall. The badly eroded and vulnerable, loose cliffs continue north-east, as does the coast path along their edge, over stiles and past a track down to Horsley Cove, once used by the fishermen of Prawle village.

Beyond large Maelcombe House *(possible accommodation),* cross an acorn stile and stream and carry on along the cliffs, over a wall stile then between high gorse bushes. The rocky path swings inland to cross a stream valley, passes a path left to Woodcombe and widens to a grassy track past buildings to reach **LANNACOMBE BEACH** *(limited parking; no facilities).*

117

From the small, sandy cove, go up through a gate onto cliffs and along a field boundary (more dangerous cliff edge). You cross marshy ground on stones and continue above The Narrows. Over sheep pasture, the path swings round a little cove and up to a wall and signpost (wrongly aligned at the author's last visit). Keep on the main path down right (not up by a fence), then veer left along cliffs on a good turfy trod.

The way becomes hemmed in by crags round Peartree Point and soon the spiky crest of **START POINT** is ahead. You climb round rocky slopes, with one steep and narrow section demanding sure footwork in windy weather, then mount gentle, brackeny slopes from which the splendid rock architecture of Start Point can be admired - great jagged buttresses supporting a ridge of pinnacles.

Attaining the ridge top at a waymark is the nearest thing to an alpine pass on the entire South West Way! Suddenly an entire new vista opens out ahead with the vast sweep of Slapton Sands and the distant Dart estuary.

Turn left along the lighthouse access road. The light, built in 1836 and with a range of 20.8 miles (33km), warns shipping off this particularly evil coastline which has caused the loss of many lives. At the road top car parking, cross a stone stile to the right and take the path through bracken; at a post, it begins a long descent of vegetated hillside and eventually emerges at Trouts Hotel *(seasonal refreshments; toilets)*.

Down a steep lane opposite can be found the remains of the old village of **HALLSANDS**. Its fate is one of the most fascinating and poignant to befall any small coastal community in the south-west peninsula. Thanks to early photographs and records, the demise of Hallsands is remarkably well documented (see especially the booklet *Hallsands - a Pictorial History* by Kathy Tanner and Peter Walsh, available locally). Briefly, the story goes thus:

Hallsands was a tiny fishing community huddled against the cliffs on a rock ledge, comprising some 40 dwellings by the mid-1800's. When the pilchard shoals declined, the inhabitants turned to crabbing and although there was no harbour, boats could be hauled up the gently shelving shingle beach which was also used for drying nets and stacking crab pots.

Not far away to the west during the last years of the 19th century, a decision was made to extend Devonport Dockyard at Keyham. Rather than pay for expensive crushed rock to be used in the project's concrete, permission was granted to Sir John Jackson's company (which had won the contract) to dredge offshore shingle in Start Bay opposite Hallsands and Beesands - shingle which legally belonged to the Crown.

From April 1897, 1,600 tonnes of shingle were removed every day from the shore between high and low water marks and it soon became clear that this was not being replaced naturally as had been expected. At a subsequent public enquiry resulting from the villagers' anxiety, Sir John successfully defended his case for the dredging to continue, maintaining that in due course the great holes in the beach would fill up with shingle swept along the bay by tidal currents.

In the winter of 1900/1, high seas destroyed the outer supporting walls and seaward properties began collapsing. A Board of Tade inspector confirmed the damage and early in 1902 the dredging license was revoked. By 1903, a Fisheries Commission report showed a 3 metre drop in beach level and warned of dire consequences if no remedial action was taken to protect the village. Compensation was granted to those losing property and public donations received. Concrete sea walls were speedily constructed with apparent success.

13 years were to pass before the final disaster struck. On 26th January 1917, a severe easterly gale and huge seas breached the sea walls, demolishing or irreparably damaging all but 1 of the 24 houses. Having denied responsibility thus far, the Board of Trade eventually paid compensation and in 1924 some of the villagers were re-housed in a small estate known as Fordworth Cottages.

The Trout sisters, descendants of a Hallsands fisherman, founded Trouts Hotel, where today you can call in for a meal or a drink. The ruined village is still an extraordinary sight, though with each winter storm more of it disappears. With care you can scramble past the gaunt gable-ends and reflect on the sea's awesome power. Even an intact house at the nearer northern end has been abandoned due to further subsidence.

From Trouts Hotel, walk down the walled pathway and up alongside a fence - a recent diversion - then go over and down behind Hallsands Hotel. The path once went in front, and in fact the building is seriously threatened by undermining; new sea defences in the form of massive blocks have been introduced. So rapidly is the sea eating away at the shoreline that guidebooks and even OS maps will certainly need future amendment!

Past some toilets, you turn left along the back of Greenstraight Beach *(summer refreshment kiosk)* where yet more rock defences have been installed. Soon the path climbs through a tunnel of undergrowth above Tinsey Head and drops to **BEESANDS** *(2 pubs; cafe/beach shop; caravan site; summer buses; car parking; toilets),* a row of seafront

Torcross, bounded by Slapton Ley and Slapton Sands

houses which were unfortunately bombed in 1943.

Just before the caravan site, go further seaward and walk between the vans - a tatty shanty town on scrubby grass and shingle, alarmingly exposed to the elements. Continue along the foreshore past Widdecombe Ley, originally dug for fishing. The coast path turns sharp left at a large white building (Beesands Cellars where pilchards were once stored) and forks up left past a telegraph pole. (If desired, you can trudge along the pebbles to Torcross at low tide.)

Making a detour inland round an old slate quarry, you continue climbing steadily through thickets and a gate to emerge by a wall, descending under telegraph wires over grass and through another gate. Just before Greyholmes Hotel, turn right and follow waymarks seawards where steps lead down to the seafront at **TORCROSS** *(pub; restaurants; cafes; shop; accommodation; summer buses for Kingsbridge and Dartmouth; telephone; car parking; toilets; early closing Saturday).*

The seafront promenade at Torcross was destroyed by storm waves in 1951, and even the solid sea walls built afterwards were breached in 1979, causing £500,000 worth of damage to properties as huge waves threw rocks and shingle at them and flooded in. The question remains whether such damage is a legacy of the Start Bay shingle dredging over three-quarters of a century ago.

Once just a small fishing hamlet surrounded by rough cattle pasture and with no coast road, Torcross is now geared to summer visitors, many of whom have come to see **SLAPTON LEY** Nature Reserve. This is Devon's largest freshwater lake, well endowed with aquatic flora which supports many insect species and, in turn, encourages birds to breed and visit the area on migrations or to overwinter. Near Slapton village is a Field Study Centre and during the summer months a programme of guided walks is offered.

A recently salvaged Sherman tank, reminder of American D-Day landing practice here, stands sentinel over the car park as we continue the coastal walking along a shingly verge seaward of the A379. If you get bored with your surroundings, passing buses can be hailed! There is no denying that the 2½ miles (4km) to Strete Gate can be unpleasant in hot, busy conditions - or delightful if traffic is light! The path grows progressively grassy and firm to the north, a graphic illustration of how vegetation consolidates the otherwise loose and unstable shingle surface - it certainly makes for easier walking!

Go straight through Slapton Sands car park *(toilets)* and on past an American war memorial. The exposed beach here is steeply shelving pebbles and shingle - much more popular with sea anglers than bathers. At the end of this long stretch, the coast road veers left at Strete Gate picnic area *(car park; toilets)*.

Owing to the line of the road and clifftop properties, there is no coast path as such for 4 miles (6km) from here to Stoke Fleming. Walking in high season traffic can be hazardous and thoroughly unenjoyable and some walkers will opt for a bus ride to the end of this section. However, in quieter conditions, the road bash does provide some good coastal views.

The onward route (at first on the course of the old road) climbs a lane ahead and up a gently graded track which narrows and steepens past a house entrance. At the main road, turn right, round a nasty bend, and into **STRETE** *(general store; pub; Post Office/shop; some accommodation; youth hostel; summer buses)*.

Continue along the road past lovely old barns at Landcombe House *(B&B)*. Beware traffic on dangerous bends! Blackpool Sands *(licensed restaurant; take away food; cream teas - all seasonal; car parking)* in its rural setting is better out of season than in and is followed by a hill to **STOKE FLEMING** *(most shops, services and accommodation; campsite; buses for Dartmouth and Kingsbridge)*.

SECTION 14 - Stoke Fleming to Brixham; 15 miles (24km)

A ferry to Kingswear and the start of an increasingly strenuous stretch of walking, recently opened, of high quality and in part 'Heritage Coast'.

Dartmouth

Sheltered pine woods lead to open clifftop at Froward Point, where the up and down work begins in earnest, round several small coves and past Scabbacombe Head to a beach reached only by footpath. Stiff climbs each side of Man Sands bring you to the southern outskirts of Brixham and a sudden transition to limestone at Berry Head. From this Site of Special Scientific Interest, the coast path makes a quick descent to the harbour at Brixham.   Grading - moderate, becoming more difficult, strenuous in places. Moderate to easy past Sharkham Point.

All shops, services and acommodation at Dartmouth and Kingswear. Once beyond Kingswear, no on-route refreshments or accommodation until Berry Head's cafe.

The coast path proper resumes east of Redlap Cove. To reach it, walk through Stoke Fleming (the church has some interesting 14th century brasses) and up a rise, forking right down a lane at the Windward Hotel, just past a speed de-restriction sign (acorn waymark). This byway bends round to cross a stream valley, undulating gently before rising to a National Trust car park at Little Dartmouth.

Devon Women's Institute and the National Trust are to be thanked for the stretch of path which now begins to the right. (If pressed for time, keep straight ahead on a short-cut bridleway to Dartmouth Castle.) Initially along by a field fence, the path veers left at a stile over

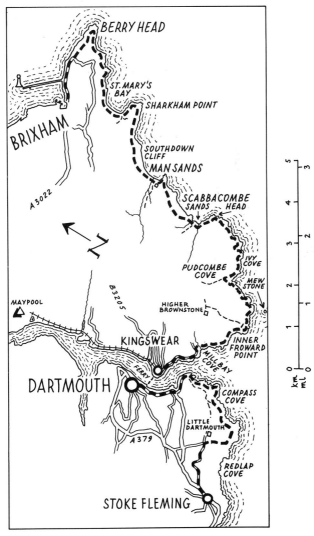

SECTION 14
STOKE FLEMING to BRIXHAM

sheep pasture parallel to a wall. Views extend right back along Start Bay.

You swing left through a wall gap, cross a footbridge and stile, to continue up alongside a fence (ignore path up left) in lush undergrowth. Passing an old telegraph cable post, you reach a stile and a rather ambiguous waymark. Take the right fork, veering back right at a bench then ahead downhill towards Compass Cove. Keep left at a stile and go down over a footbridge which spans a rocky chasm ending in a dramatic cave.

Now the path is delightfully close to sea and rocks as it rounds Blackstone Point and reveals the Dart estuary with grey Kingswear Castle on the far shore. Up through luxuriant woods, the way reaches a lane at a rose-covered cottage. (The short-cut bridleway from Little Dartmouth joins here.)

In 10m, the coast path turns right, down into trees and along the trod nearest the lane wall, emerging onto the lane itself which you follow down *(car parking)*. Dartmouth Castle is situated below to the right, a 15th century defence against French raiders and, with Kingswear Castle across the river, capable of blocking the channel with a chain during times of war. Nearby is St. Petroc's Church and a summer ferry to Dartmouth quay.

First views ahead are of house-covered valley slopes and a busy waterway. At the bottom road junction, keep straight on, round the back of a small cove and into **DARTMOUTH** *(all shops, services and accommodation; youth hostel; Tourist Information; ferries; boat trips; Royal Navy College; bus services; early closing Wednesday/Saturday).*

Already a significant deep water port by the 12th century, Dartmouth has a long maritime tradition which its Naval College continues. Departure point for the 2nd and 3rd Crusades, the port flourished during the Middle Ages as continental trade increased and its prosperity was boosted by the opening up of the Newfoundland fishing banks in the 1600's. Today, like Salcombe to the west, it is a premier yachting centre, though altogether a busier place, with its vehicle ferries, naval associations and the Torbay Steam Railway which runs during the summer season between Paignton and Kingswear quayside (connections with British Rail main line services).

NOTE: The ensuing 11 miles (18km) round Scabbacombe Head to Brixham contain some hefty gradients and surprisingly rugged terrain. There are no refreshment or accommodation points at all until the outskirts of Brixham are reached, so walkers are advised to carry adequate food and drink and to allow plenty of time for the hike. You will not be disappointed by the scenery, which in part has been desig-

nated 'Heritage Coast' and which represents the last really wild
stretch of high quality coastline for many a mile to the east.

Of the 3 ferries across the Dart, walkers will normally use the lower
one from the central quay across to Kingswear. It operates 7 days a
week all year round, every 6 minutes in summer, every 12 minutes in
winter, and from 7.00am. (8.00am. Sundays) to 10.55pm.

Walk up the slipway at **KINGSWEAR** *(shops, services and accommodation)* and turn right down the road. In 50m you pass through an arch
and turn left up Alma Steps, then right, along a lane past houses and
palm trees with good views over to Dartmouth Castle. Keep straight
on along this leafy lane and down past some flats and garages and the
entrance to Kingswear Court (waymark).

Until quite recently, no coast path had been negotiated round
Scabbacombe Head, dictating a road walk to Man Sands. Much of the
new path is dedicated to the memory of the late Lt.Co. Jones, a Falk-
land Islands VC over whose estate it passes. To join it, in about 100m
turn right at a sign to Froward Point and Warren Wood, down
wooden steps and on down grassy hillside. Cross a track, descend
more steps, over a stream and turn right along the track for 15m.
Opposite a turreted old mill (in a dangerous condition at the time of
writing) turn up left on a steep path into lovely Warren Woods above
Mill Bay Cove.

Passing some impressive conifers and an acorn sign on firebeaters,
there are fine views of the estuary dotted with yachts, ferries, launches
and pleasure cruisers. In summer sunshine, the scent of pine resin, the
deep shade and luxuriant growth all conspire to evoke the Mediter-
ranean coast.

Beyond a National Trust sign for Higher Brownstone *(car park)*, the
way drops and climbs through the woods (ignore a path up left), with
some steeper gradients leading out to old wartime bunkers on **INNER
FROWARD POINT**. A very necessary signpost unravels the paths:
main coast path to the right, a short-cut link straight on, Higher
Brownstone car park left. As other signs declare, this is also a nature
reserve.

The main route goes right, down brick steps, looping round the
point itself. (The link path zig-zags down through bracken to meet it.)
Offshore, the Mew Stone is smothered in guano from its frenetic
colonies of seabirds. There is a stiff climb back up to clifftop woods at
a bench and waymark post leading ahead.

Suddenly you are out in the open above a field corner (path left to
viewpoint). Proceed ahead, dropping towards the Mew Stone; once
round a corner, the next stretch of unspoiled, virgin coast is revealed,

125

indented and tortuous. As might be expected, the path snakes up and down, in and out, establishing a character which is sustained for the next 6 miles (10km) or so.

Ascending by zig-zags through bracken to a sign (left to car park), you turn right for Pudcombe Cove, cross a stile and go down through woods. Turn sharp right at a post and go ahead onto a tarmac pathway past rhododendrons. 10m before a gate, turn right over a stream above the cove and head back towards the sea. Steps lead out onto rough, open hillside above a tiny inlet, then the path climbs round by a wall corner to another waymark sign (another path left to car park) where you keep ahead for Scabbacombe Sands.

Soon you are plunging downhill above Ivy Cove and round a corner to confront high, silver-grey cliffs whose flanks you climb in zig-zags, with views far ahead to Lyme Bay in good weather. Still on switch-back gradients, you drop right in numerous twists over grassy cliffside - with the knowledge by now that height lost has to be regained! The first sighting ahead of Berry Head's limestone prow may lighten flagging spirits as the path climbs to a low wall and National Trust 'Coleton' sign on **SCABBACOMBE HEAD.**

Descending steeply (awkward in wet weather), you reach the back of Scabbacombe Sands *(no amenities)*, cross a footbridge and climb out the other side. However, there is an unseen depression to pass before the real legwork begins. *(Scabbacombe car park 600m up left.)* From a stile at the top, you walk along flat clifftop field edges round Crabrock

The Mew Stone from Inner Froward Point

Point - a welcome respite from recent big ups and downs! Drop to a stile and keep at first along the top of pasture before going down the middle towards a concrete manhole cover. You pass behind Coastguard cottages (this must have been a tempting location for smugglers!) and at the bottom track turn left and immediately right down steps to the limekiln at **MAN SANDS** *(no amenities)* - used in the days when coasters unloaded local limestone here.

Walk along the back of this isolated and rather inaccessible beach and up steps to begin the relentless 420ft. (128m) climb of Southdown Cliff. Keeping seaward, the red earth path crosses a stream and continues out round Sharkham Point. You emerge on a track, turning down right towards Berry Head. Just before reaching an open space, turn left up steps past a breeze-block wall, whereafter the path climbs round to a viewpoint above **ST. MARY'S BAY.**

Already, the holiday building development which dominates eastward walking round most of Torbay is near at hand. At a gate (acorn on wall), turn right down a concrete path. Where the steps divide, turn left outside the perimeter fence of a holiday bungalow estate; there are few views here in summer due to foliage.

Up through cattle pasture and over the seaward of 2 stiles, the coast path flanks a chalet park and enters **BERRY HEAD COUNTRY PARK.** The official guide to Berry Head is worth purchasing (possibly from car park kiosk or cafe), for there is much to see here - fulmars and auks nesting on the cliffs *(pay telescope)*, also perhaps gannets diving for fish and the antics of other seabirds; limestone-tolerant plants and a nature trail; the Coastguard Station and lighthouse; an old limestone quarry; and the fortifications which were built in 1803 during the Napoleonic Wars when an invasion by Napoleon Bonaparte was feared but never materialised.

In fact, Berry Head's flora and fauna habitats have been made a Site of Special Scientific Interest and a Site of Special Protection. Of special interest to the coastal walker may well be the extensive views from this headland - sometimes as far as Portland Bill in Dorset.

The seaward path meets the fort walls, turning left on a stony track alongside. Out by the car park, you cross green turf ahead then traverse overgrown heathland out onto open grass *(turn right for Fort Cafe -snacks, meals, drinks, etc.)*. The coast path is signed along the track then seaward past a metal fence and gate, with excellent views over Brixham breakwater. Drop through woods and turn right down the lane past Berry Head Hotel, continuing along the road into **BRIXHAM** *(all shops, services and accommodation; campsite; Tourist Information; museum; buses; summer ferry to Torquay; boat trips, etc;*

Torbay from Brixham breakwater

early closing Wednesday).

Brixham's fishermen claimed to have discovered the North Sea fishing grounds in the mid-19th century. Somewhat earlier, and commemorated by a statue, William of Orange landed here in 1688 with 30,000 men on his way to becoming King William III. Brixham has turned increasingly to tourism over recent years, though its busy harbour has lost none of its character. The replica of the 'Golden Hind' is moored at the quayside when not at sea, adding a splash of colour and historical interest to the crush of fishing and pleasure craft.

SECTION 15 - Brixham to Torquay Harbour;   8 miles (13km)

After a promising start, an increasingly urban walk with little to recommend it other than the amenities it passes and the constant sea views. Options exist to take the summer ferry or a bus, either the whole way from Brixham, or from Goodrington where the official coast path ends.   Grading - moderate (with a few steep climbs) to Goodrington. Easy to Torquay Harbour.
Refreshments at Broad Sands. All shops, services and accommodation at Paignton and beyond.

Brixham stands at the southern end of Tor Bay. This great sweep of sheltered coast, with Torquay as its focal point, enjoys an exceptionally mild climate and during the 19th century developed as a retreat for invalids, particularly those afflicted with consumption. Others, denied continental travel by the onset of the Napoleonic Wars, looked

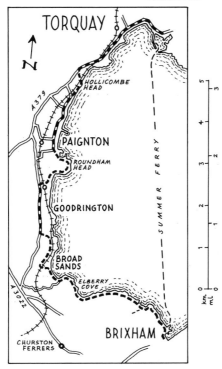

SECTION 15
BRIXHAM to TORQUAY HARBOUR

to Torquay as a kind of surrogate French Riviera or Bay of Naples. Indeed, new buildings were given an Italian appearance by astute property developers, enhancing the resort's appeal to would-be 'Grand Tourers'. Princess Victoria and her mother added the royal seal of approval by their visit in 1833 and Torquay's ascendancy as a fashionable holiday destination was assured.

By 1848 the railway had reached Torquay and had opened up the area to many more thousands of visitors. Later, following the advent of Bank Holidays and paid leave from work, South Devon's holiday industry was to grow apace. In 1968, Torquay, Paignton and Brixham joined forces, nominally at least, to become Torbay, a virtually contiguous resort occupying 20 miles (32km) of coastline.

Today, Torbay's 'Riviera' image persists - a blend of palm trees and balmy air, of gently shelving beaches and calm seas, of prolific accommodation and a lively entertainments scene. However, unless based here, the coastal walker may not list such attractions in his priorities. Many will be taking to the coast path specifically to escape crowds and traffic and the appeal of stomping along pavements may be shortlived, however distracting the surroundings.

Coast path purists will no doubt wish to tread every metre of available shoreline, and the following text will assist in the achievement of this. But apart from the occasional pleasant interlude, there is not a great deal to recommend the urban walking from Goodrington, through Torquay itself to Babbacombe. With railway and road cheek by jowl with the shore virtually the whole way from Teignmouth to

The 'Golden Hind' replica in Brixham harbour

the Exe estuary, some might claim (the author among them) that really worthwhile coastal walking does not resume until Exmouth is reached (walking east).

In the circumstances it is less easy to advocate quality day walks on this heavily developed stretch of coast, and long-distance walkers might well be advised to take public transport over the worst bits - especially if time is limited. The summer ferry to Torquay Harbour makes a useful short-cut, for example.

To continue the walking route from Brixham Harbour, go along the north quayside and up Overgang Road, turning right along Blackball Lane at the top of a rise *(toilets)*. Go down across Freshwater Quarry car park to seaward of the Freshwater Cafe. The path leads along and up steps through a park, emerging onto the road at Brixham Bay Holiday Park.

Keep forward on a clear path (signed Churston Ferrers) and at a metal stile turn right down steps though woods and round the back of pebbly Churston Cove. Climb a flight of steps up the ridge between cove and sea - these take you to an easy path between a golf course fence and trees above the sea. After a mile or so, go through a brick gateway and down through trees and steps to Elberry Cove, a popular location for water skiing.

Once along the pebbly beach and up steps at the far end, the coast path veers right above low, rocky cliffs, out across a broad, grassy headland and round past benches to a metal railing and the beach huts of **BROAD SANDS** *(refreshments; telephone; car park; toilets; Maypool youth hostel approx. 2½ (4km) - south-east inland).*

Walk right along the sea wall and just before the cliffs start at the northern end of the beach huts, turn left up a tarmac pathway, under the railway viaduct *(the Torbay Steam Railway runs between Kingswear and Paignton)* and immediately right up steps. Continuing alongside the railway fence, steps lead down and you pass between the railway track and a large caravan site. Keep straight on over the site track, past an old semaphore signal, up steps and behind a bungalow and apartments to a side road. Turn left to the main A379 road and right along it at **GOODRINGTON**. Since shops, services and accommodation exist in abundance, no specific listings will be made.

There is no official coast path onwards from here to Hope's Nose, east of Torquay. Buses are frequent, but you can walk to Torquay Harbour without any difficulties. Go along Goodrington seafront and up to Roundham Gardens on a twisting path, circumventing the headland to Cliff Road and along to Paignton Harbour. Where Paignton promenade swings left beneath the railway, there is a path up to little

Hollicombe Head. Although by turning right it is possible to walk through part of a park here (the former gasworks!), you are soon back on the seafront road which is followed round to **TORQUAY HARBOUR** *(all shops, services and accommodation; Tourist Information; British Rail station; coach station; summer ferry to Brixham; museum; etc; early closing Wednesday/Saturday).*

SECTION 16 - Torquay Harbour to Exmouth;   16 miles (26km)

A long walk but much easier over the latter half and with numerous options to take public transport. The initial scenic progression of promenade, gardens and open spaces with good sea views leads round the northern headland of Tor Bay and into less urbanised surroundings. Undulating through woods and past a limestone promontory quarry, the path crosses downland before descending to the small harbour resort of Babbacombe. A steep climb past a cliff railway is followed by more largely wooded terrain, dipping and climbing and including a spectacular cliffside ledge path towards Maidencombe. The next stretch contains some fierce gradients, but beyond Labrador Bay the going is mostly level. You cross the Teign River by ferry, proceeding past Teignmouth and Dawlish either by beach and sea wall or road, depending on tides. From Dawlish Warren, a short stretch of road walking takes you to Starcross and the ferry for Exmouth.   Grading - moderate to Babbacombe. More difficult to Labrador Bay. Mostly easy to Starcross.

Pub and seasonal refreshments at Babbacombe; ditto at Maidencombe. Refreshments, shops, services and accommodation at Shaldon. All shops, services and accommodation at Teignmouth and Dawlish, including British Rail stations. Refreshments and amenities at Dawlish Warren. Pub at Cockwood. 4 pubs at Starcross.

NOTE: The main concern of this guidebook is with the official long-distance South West Way route. For comprehensive details of other walks in this popular holiday area, consult the booklet *Torbay Coast Paths*, available locally, and other relevant publications. The South West Way Association's leaflet *Brixham to Labrador Bay* contains a wealth of background information which lies outside the scope of this general guidebook.

From Torquay Harbour you have to divert slightly inland from the waterfront, up past the Imperial Hotel, to reach Peaked Tor Cove, whereafter a good up-and-down path takes you to open ground on Daddyhole Plain. At Meadfoot Beach you emerge onto Marine Drive. Turn right on a path above the shore opposite Thatcher Rock - now back on the official coast path - which leads out round spectacular

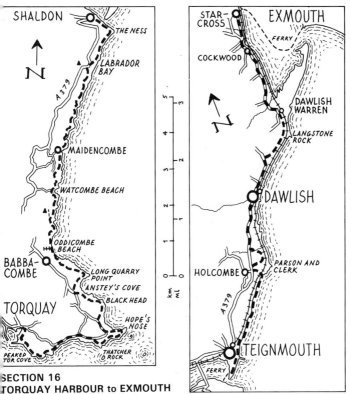

SECTION 16
TORQUAY HARBOUR to EXMOUTH

Hope's Nose with its cluster of offshore rock islands and seabird colonies.

Walking along Marine Drive (actually above it) for about 500m, take a path off right - Bishop's Walk - which goes round the rocky Black Head and into wooded Anstey's Cove at a car park *(refreshments)*. 150m along the road, steps and another path branch off to the right towards the pinnacled limestone of Long Quarry Point, over Walls Hill and down to the beach and small quay at **BABBACOMBE** *(pub; summer refreshments; shops; car park; toilets)*.

There now follows a sea level walk along to Oddicombe Beach *(summer refreshments)* where the way climbs from the lower station to

133

pass beneath the fascinating cliff railway. The steep path to Petit Tor Point levels off in dense woodland, crosses the access lane to Watcombe Beach and continues up the other side on welcome steps. Passing a wooded glen and an airy cliffside ledge equipped with a handrail, you are approaching picturesque **MAIDENCOMBE**: a recent path improvement avoids road walking on Rockhouse Lane by turning down towards the sea and reaching the village at a car park above the beach *(summer refreshments; pub; limited accommodation; telephone; car park; toilets)*.

It is only 1½ miles (2.5km) to Labrador Bay, but a tough little walk it proves to be as the path dips and climbs through a series of steep hanging valleys. Sea views are rather limited due to foliage in the thickets and fields passed through on this switchback section close to the cliff edge.

Follow the road to the cliffs at the north end of Maidencombe Beach and almost immediately the legwork begins between Blackallers and Mackerel coves. Eventually you are forced by clifftop buildings to veer steeply up inland to the busy A379 road at **LABRADOR BAY** *(car park)*. However, watch for a path off right very soon - it drops to the bottom edge of a field and follows the lower side of a pitch and putt course where coast path signs resume, leading you round The Ness *(car park)*. Turn left and drop straightforwardly with fine views of red sandstone cliffs to **SHALDON** *(shops, services and accommodation, including campsite; frequent coastal buses from Shaldon Bridge; ferry to Teignmouth; early closing Thursday)*.

To cross the River Teign, catch the ferry from the Marine Drive foreshore. It runs every 20 minutes during the following operating periods:- Easter to the beginning of May - 8.00am. to 6.00pm. Throughout May - 8.00am. to 7.00pm. Throughout June - 8.00am. to 8.00pm. Early July - 8.00am. to 9.00pm. Mid-July to end of August - 8.00am. to 10.00pm. September and October - 8.00am. to dusk (10.00am. start on Sundays). November to Easter - 8.00am. to 5.00pm. weekdays only. Enquiries tel: 79770.

Having disembarked from the ferry, walk along the seafront past the pier at **TEIGNMOUTH** *(all shops, services and accommodation; Tourist Information; frequent coastal buses; British Rail station; early closing Thursday)*. One of south Devon's oldest settlements, Teignmouth possesses all the characteristics of the archetypal English seaside - a long promenade, a pier, a safe sandy beach, entertainment for children and adults alike and a pleasant old town, despite damage by German hit-and-run raids during the last war. Exports of pottery ball clay leave the port for Europe.

The River Teign ferry

Teignmouth

An official coast path as such does not exist here, but once again it is possible to find your way forward, mostly close to the sea. At low tide the promenade then the sea wall can be followed northwards, but the wall ends near a railway tunnel at the Parson and Clerk's headland and the only option to continue is under the railway line. This becomes flooded at high water, necessitating a time-consuming detour to the road.

If progress here is clear, climb Smugglers Lane to Windward Lane at **HOLCOMBE** *(pubs; buses)* - unfortunately on the busy A379 for 150m before turning right. A loop avoiding the road (watch carefully for signs) now keeps along by a hedge, back to the cliff edge, across 2 fields and veering left to steps and the old Teignmouth Road.

Walk down into **DAWLISH** *(all shops, services and accommodation; Tourist Information; British Rail station; early closing Thursday)*, originally a farming village inland which was developed seawards during the last century. All along this stretch of coast, trains on the main Paddington to Penzance line run between sheer cliffs and the sea, often on a sea wall embankment. This audacious engineering project of the mid-1800's was the brainchild of Isambard Kingdom Brunel and provides rail travellers with one of Britain's most exhilarating rides - particularly in rough weather when the carriages are covered in sea spray.

You can walk along the beach to Dawlish Warren at low tide; at high tide, turn inland over a footbridge just past the station and on along the coast road. Where it swings inland, fork off right by the Rockstone Hotel - a short official path section past the red bulk of Langstone Rock and out to **DAWLISH WARREN** *(shops and refreshments; amenities on caravan park; car park; toilets; railway station)*. This popular family resort with a good sandy beach lies at the western end of a large, vegetated sand spit in the Exe estuary, well known for its flora and fauna and a designated nature reserve *(museum)* as well as a golf course!

NOTE: If walking outside the main summer season (ie. before May or after September), you will be faced with a dilemma. Unable to use the summer-only ferry to Exmouth, you could attempt to procure a boat owner willing to take you across (duly recompensed, it is hoped!). Alternatively you could walk further up the Exe banks to the year-round Topsham ferry (daily 8.00am. to 5.30pm. during October to April. 8.00am. to 8.00pm. May to September. No Tuesday service. Frequency according to demand and subject to tide and weather). Even this option leaves you with a less than satisfactory road and overgrown path route back south to Exmouth.

Many off-season walkers will simply take the train or bus to Exeter and along the Exe's east bank to Exmouth: services are not too frequent however, so pre-checking is advised.

Assuming the Starcross ferry is running, walk along the road past Cockwood *(pub)* to the pier *(car parking)* - a distance of some 2 miles (3km). The ferry service is 7 days a week, from 10.00am. to 12.00 noon then 1.00pm. to 5.45pm. - summer only, usually from 1st May to end September. For enquiries phone (0626) 862452. **STARCROSS** village has 4 pubs and the oldest sailing club in Britain, founded in the 1700's. The Atmospheric Railway pub is named after Brunel's revolutionary - but eventually aborted - air-driven railway.

15 minutes later you will alight on the ferry steps at the bustling town of **EXMOUTH**. Popular since the early 18th century thanks to its long sandy beach, Exmouth remains a family resort and water sports location. It is also a sizeable commercial centre for the area with its own docks. With all shops, *(early closing Wednesday)*, services and accommodation and good transport links with Exeter, Exmouth makes a good starting or finishing point for coastal walking. All the troublesome river estuaries lie to the west, so eastward travel is unimpeded. Although still dotted with seaside resorts, the coast ahead reverts to a more natural character, allowing the walker access to unspoiled scenery once again.

CHAPTER 3
Exmouth to Poole Harbour
(99 miles - 159km)

Passing a vast caravan park and a Royal Marines firing range, the coast path climbs over high ground to genteel Budleigh Salterton, detouring inland for a river crossing and regaining the red sandstone cliffs along to Ladram Bay. A stiff climb ensues over wooded High Peak to reach the delightful town of Sidmouth. The going is rough and strenuous through big combes to Branscombe Mouth, where an old landslip is traversed to the small resort of Beer.

Easy walking to Seaton precedes a 6 mile (10km) stretch through the biggest of the south coast landslips, now 130 years old and luxuriantly overgrown. Historic Lyme Regis, with its famous Cobb, is separated from Charmouth by badly eroding cliffs for which a detour is necessary. Beyond, you climb Golden Cap, the south coast's highest top, whereafter rolling cliffs bring you past Seatown to West Bay, once Bridport's harbour.

The great pebble ridge of Chesil Bank stretches from Burton Beach 18 miles (29km) to Portland, for most of the way shadowed by the coast path, first to ancient Abbotsbury, famous for its Swannery and tithe barn, then briefly inland before returning to the shores of The Fleet Nature Reserve, a lagoon separating the Chesil from the mainland. With direct public transport options available to Weymouth, you approach the town past a firing range and through increasingly less attractive surroundings to Portland Harbour.

Small holiday settlements on Weymouth Bay are replaced past Osmington Mills by the first in a succession of high chalk cliffs whose scenery includes Durdle Door and the much-visted Lulworth Cove. Army firing ranges determine the times of public access, but the onward coast path to Swanage is one of the South West Way's most sensational stages. Very strenuous but dramatically rewarding, these steeply rolling cliffs pass the 'ghost village' of Tyneham, then an oil well and extensive rock ledges at Kimmeridge. Still energetic, the way passes seaward of the lovely old village of Worth Matravers and reaches St. Aldhelm's Head, with its Norman chapel. Limestone cliff

Exmouth seafront

quarries punctuate the wild coast between here and the lighthouse on Anvil Point where country park tracks lead to the family resort of Swanage.

Over Ballard Down and past Old Harry Rocks, you leave Studland village for the last few miles along a sandy beach to South Haven Point and the ferry for Sandbanks on Poole Harbour.

SECTION 17 - Exmouth to Sidmouth; 12 miles (19km)

Exmouth's long promenade leads to an easy cliff walk over to the vast caravan town and nearby firing range at Sandy Bay. A gradual climb over West Down Beacon on high, landslipped cliffs above a pebble beach brings you to the genteel little resort of Budleigh Salterton. Detouring briefly inland to cross the River Otter, a straightforward path follows the cliff edge to another holiday park at Ladram Bay with its sensational offshore sea stacks. A stiff climb ensues to wooded High Peak and over Peak Hill, finally descending to the seafront at Sidmouth.   Grading - easy to Sandy Bay, then moderate, with one or two steep climbs.

Refreshments in summer at Sandy Bay. All shops, services and accommodation at Budleigh Salterton. Seasonal refreshments at Ladram Bay.

Walk all along Exmouth's seafront with wide views back round Tor Bay to Berry Head. The River Exe floods into the sea, creating

139

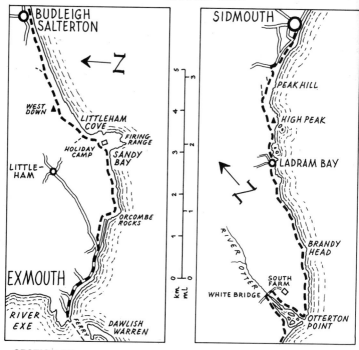

SECTION 17
EXMOUTH to SIDMOUTH

hazardous bathing conditions, but the sands and dunes are popular - witness the rows of beach huts.

At a car park and red brick cafe *(summer refreshments; toilets)*, either continue along the promenade to Orcombe Rocks and climb steps to join the coast path, or walk behind the car park then up Foxholes Hill (the official routing). In 200m, the tarmac pathway turns off right between bushes (sign for Budleigh Salterton 4 miles) outside clifftop properties and out along open field edges on High Land of Orcombe, 250ft. (76m) above the sea.

With no equivocation, the way soon approaches **SANDY BAY** - an incredible expanse of caravans and without doubt the biggest site passed on the South West Way. At first you skirt outside the wooden perimeter fence, then walk round past a bar/restaurant and up along the inland edge of a Royal Marines firing range. No more incongru-

'The Floors' from above Littleham Cove

ous a juxtaposition exists anywhere along the coast path: the clatter of small arms fire punctuates the business of holidaymaking and the 2 establishments do make the most unlikely bedfellows!

Crossing the grassy slopes of the caravan town, you pass an access path to Littleham Cove, now too dangerous to use due to subsidence at the bottom. Nevertheless there is a splendid view of the arc of steeply shelving pebbly beach below high and overgrown landslipped cliffs known as The Floors. It is interesting to recall that back past Straight Point range the beaches are sandy.

Passing a path left for Littleham (¾ mile - 1,200m) and a little wooded dell with a footbridge, the coast path rises gently through gorse with wide all-round views. Doubling back near the top, you reach West Down Beacon (423ft. - 129m), its trig. pillar all but concealed in bracken. Keep straight on outside the golf course chain-link fence, descending gently past many benches and through pine woods. Stay ahead at a post, ignoring a path off left. The way soon becomes surfaced along hedged clifftop, crosses a grassy field and enters a narrow lane waymarked down past flats to the seafront at **BUDLEIGH SALTERTON** *(all shops, services and accommodation; Tourist Information; museum; buses; car parks; early closing Thursday).* For the town centre, turn left by the toilets, otherwise continue along

The mouth of the River Otter

the prom past man-powered capstans used to haul fishing boats up the steep beach.

Sir Walter Raleigh was born nearby at the farmhouse of Hayes Barton and Millais' famous painting 'The Boyhood of Raleigh' uses this seafront as its setting. Budleigh Salterton's origins lie in the working of salt pans at the mouth of the River Otter around 700 years ago. Later it became an exclusive watering place for the well-to-do - an identity which, though faded, is still discernible today in the absence of common entertainments and exploitative development. Though the shelving beach is not ideal for bathing, it does yield a great variety of coloured pebbles.

Where the seafront road rises, keep ahead on the pedestrian prom past beach huts *(summer refreshments; toilets)* to a coast path finger post. Although empowered to do so, the Countryside Commission has yet to provide a footbridge over the mouth of the River Otter. At very low tides and after a long dry spell, it may be possible to wade across, but the channel is deep and the general advice is not to try. This means a detour upstream to White Bridge and back to the coast - an extra mile or more.

You now aim for the far right corner of the large car park, where you will pass a bench and find a path into the Otter Estuary Reserve (Devon Wildlife Trust). This starts above a sports field and pavilion, using the top of a flood embankment. In 1km, turn right across White

Bridge but ignore the obvious riverside path. Swing right instead on the farm lane, over a cattle-grid and immediately right along a field edge. *(South Farm shop is 300m along the lane - open daily including Sundays.)*

Crossing a reedy stream, you continue seawards between fields and estuary bank conifers. A 'Dangerous to cross river' notice by a war-time bunker will confirm most walkers' judgement at having made the detour, but it is worth pausing for the fine perspective over the Otter mouth and Budleigh Salterton.

Here at Otterton Point, the coast path veers left and follows the top of high, striated red-sandstone cliffs whose base has been undermined by wave action. The going is pleasant, affording views inland as well as to sea as you skirt arable land above Black Head and Brandy Head, the latter no doubt associated with smuggling which was rife during the 18th and 19th centuries.

Passing a derelict building, the lofty wooded hump of High Peak rears ahead, with distant Sidmouth cradled between red cliffs beyond. Stiles lead on and you descend, crossing a stream and the beach slipway to arrive at **LADRAM BAY** *(Three Rocks Inn - seasonal meals, snacks and drinks; telephone; toilets)*. Another caravan town, though smaller than Sandy Bay's, is situated behind the little wooded valley. Just off the rather cramped beach here are several spectacular sea stacks, sculpted by wind and waves.

Staying round the edge of grassy banks, the coast path leaves this

The view from Brandy Head, High Peak centre top

Sidmouth seafront

holidaymaking location at a stile just above the swimming pool. There follows a considerable climb of over 400ft. (130m), first up a field edge then up steps into a Forestry Commission conifer plantation (fire risk) at the top of which the gradient levels off. This is **HIGH PEAK,** but the path contours round its northern flanks as a fire break and you would need to take one of the paths up right to reach the summit trig. pillar. Views from there are quite superb in good conditions.

Emerging from the woods, turn right round a depression and along the top field edge to a stile. After a narrow stretch by a field fence to another stile, you reach a path junction. Take the right fork (recently improved for better sea views) up Peak Hill. Once over the top, drop through thin woodland and turn right at a path junction to enter mature deciduous woods and finish the descent to Peak Hill Road down steps. Turn right and soon you will find a broad grassy slope angling down alongside the road all the way into **SIDMOUTH** *(all shops, services and accommodation; Tourist Information; buses; Inshore Rescue Boat; car parks; early closing Thursday).*

With nearly 500 listed buildings in its midst, little wonder that Sidmouth is an architectural gem. Adopted as a desirable spot by the wealthy and refined around the turn of the 18th and 19th centuries, the town is composed largely of houses which characterise that era. Its spacious, shady gardens have a similar genteel maturity, yet the shopping streets are varied and lively, catering for a wide range of visitors.

SECTION 18 - Sidmouth to Seaton; 9 miles (14km)

No great distance but a fairly demanding walk, especially from Sidmouth to Branscombe Mouth; the increasingly rough path switchbacks through big combes between sea level and the 500ft. (150m) contour. Waymarking is poor towards the end of this stretch. There follows either a climb over Britain's westernmost chalk cliffs or an undulating route through a spectacular overgrown landslip to the popular little resort of Beer. Now thoroughly back in civilisation, an easy pathway and shingle beach lead to

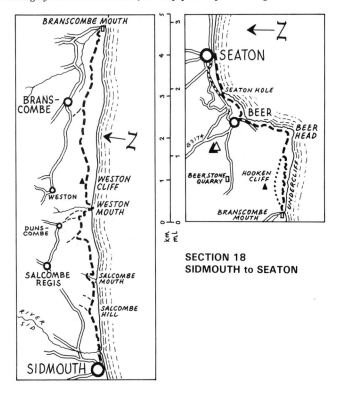

SECTION 18
SIDMOUTH to SEATON

145

the seafront at Seaton. Grading - strenuous to Branscombe Mouth; moderate to Seaton.
Refreshments at Branscombe Mouth. All shops, services and accommodation at Beer.

NOTE: Between Sidmouth and Branscombe Mouth - about 6 miles (10km) - there are some hefty downs-and-ups over surprisingly rough terrain for the south Devon coast. This stretch is quite remote, with no refreshment points and walkers should allow at least 3 hours, longer in adverse weather or if heavily laden.

Leave Sidmouth by walking all along the seafront, past the Inshore Rescue Boathouse and crossing the River Sid on an ornate footbridge where steps begin the ascent of Salcombe Hill. At first you go up past benches and domestic gardens into National Trust property where views begin to open out as height is gained. The overgrown cliffs support many bird and plant species and are a nature conservation area.

Up through a low copse, steps lead into hillside woods. At a path junction (confusing waymark arrow pointing between paths), keep left on a stepped path up through trees to a finger post. Here on **SALCOMBE HILL** an exceptionally wide panorama extends over the Sid valley, developed inland to Sidford, and the coast. On the way up, the underlying rocks have changed from soft red marl to a durable sandstone called greensand, better suited to heath and conifer plantation than to normal agricultural use.

Turning right *(straight on to car park)*, you reach a National Trust collecting box, where timber steps provide access to a viewing table. (Note the beacon nearby.) Just through the clifftop handgate stands a stone tablet inscribed 'South Combe Farm, including the cliff summit of Salcombe Hill dedicated by the owner as a permanent open space. Vaughan Cornish 1937. No sounds or worldly toil ascending there mar the full burst of prayer'.

Flat walking follows to a handgate and the start of a big descent. As the coast path veers right, down steps (ignore path off left), one can reflect on how well it is built - even benches are provided - compared with less popular stretches. Steps are better than a potentially muddy slither, but there are many of them! Reaching the edge of rough pasture, continue on down to where a path off right descends 130 steps to Salcombe Mouth: unless seeking a secluded beach, you will be relieved to note the coast path swinging left inland above the overgrown stream ravine.

In 200m the way turns right over a footbridge (straight on to

Salcombe Regis ½ mile), then back towards the cliff edge, veering left up the seaward boundary of rough grazing. Over a stile, the path becomes much steeper through bracken and the final 200ft. (60m) are quite strenuous, slippery in wet weather and near the cliff edge.

At the top (500ft. - 152m), the National Trust's Higher Dunscombe property is entered and for a while the going is easy along another in this series of flat-topped hills. Chalk begins to outcrop in the cliffs about half-way along and soon appears in the path too - a foretaste of the limestone to be encountered from Beer Head eastwards.

As the next descent begins, you swing inland (waymarked), while far below waves break on the pebbly foreshore beneath vegetated cliff-falls. In a few hundred metres, the path drops right, into the top of a tiny valley. Over the stile, go into the spinney, up steps and out onto a broad path at a National Trust collecting box. Keeping right, the way winds pleasantly along the level before descending into woods. At a waymark post (left to Dunscombe ⅓ mile), turn down right on a shady but sometimes extremely slippery path, out into the open down an awkward muddy channel between gorse and bracken, and on down to the bottom of pastureland.

Here you turn right (another path left to Dunscombe) into a nature reserve. Steps take you right down to the shingly beach at **WESTON MOUTH,** once used by fishermen whose shacks have been converted into holiday chalets. Cross the stream and in 50m turn up left just past 'The Glen'. Steps climb back to pasture level (straight on for Weston, ⅔ mile) and the coast path strikes half-right diagonally uphill (not in the direction of a finger post). As you climb, take a glance or two back to the chalky bastions of cliff above wild, overgrown landslips. These are some of the highest cliffs on the path and are virtually untouched by man.

Steps and stiles lead you up very rugged hillside - a mixture of nettles, bracken and brambles - emerging to the right of the summit trig. pillar on **WESTON CLIFF** (531ft. - 162m). This lonely and more demanding stretch continues on the level, close to the sheer edge in places, and passes a path left to Weston village *(telephone)*. At an askew finger post (many have been vandalised hereabouts), the coast path angles half-left away from the sea and crosses a shallow depression. From a field corner stile beyond, enter the big field ahead and go round its seaward edge.

At the author's last visit, waymarking was scanty from now on, but it is anticipated that Devon County Council will soon provide a new path line nearer the sea.

Out of the big field, walk along parallel to the hedge on the left, continuing through the next field too, at the end of which is a gate in the left corner. Go through and turn right onto a farm track between hedges. This opens out after the next field gate, where you carry on ahead (ignore an acorn post pointing down left into woods - the main coast path arrow missing). Stay on the track, past overgrown flint waste mounds from previous lime-burning, and keep left at a fork, with Branscombe village now glimpsed between trees to the left.

Potentially very muddy, the track narrows to a grassy path and climbs through woodland to a National Trust sign for West Cliff. Straight on at first, the path eventually drops left by bracken, goes through a handgate and down a field, turning right along below houses to **BRANSCOMBE MOUTH** *(beach shop, including groceries; licensed restaurant/cafe; car park; toilets)*. Facilities here owe their existence to road access for holidaymakers (the first since Sidmouth) and a nearby caravan park. Old Branscombe village, lying up the valley to the north-west, contains an interesting church of Saxon origin, thatched cottages and a pub - the Mason's Arms.

Cross the stream mouth, where a coast path stile provides access to East Cliff. Angling uphill, you meet the caravan park track and a choice of two forward routes: a straightforward, though steep, climb over Hooken Cliff for wide coastal views, or the more varied undercliff option. For the clifftop path simply climb up to the left; for the undercliff path turn right into the caravan park entrance - the route now described.

There have been many major landslips on this part of the British coast within geologically recent times. This one is an early example, having occurred in March 1790 and involving some 10 acres of collapsed cliff. Large stabilised landslips, re-colonised with flora and fauna, are of special interest to naturalists, but minor ones are a continual threat to farmland and property, not to mention the coast path itself!

In the caravan park, keep to the main left-hand track and watch for a signed path off to the right on a small hill. This weaves tortuously through the vegetated undercliff beneath soaring, striated rock faces, still vaguely menacing. After more sinuous windings, the path climbs in earnest and exciting zig-zags lead up near the precipitous edge. Looking back you will see the Pinnacles and an adit in the cliff face (not a natural cave) associated with Beer stone quarry to the north.

At a stile you meet the clifftop path and turn right to Britain's most westerly chalk headland - **BEER HEAD** - and a marvellous viewpoint over the landslip. Ahead lies the long sweep of Seaton Beach and the unmistakable, if distant, profile of Portland Bill. Follow the cliff edge along field bottoms and at a gate join a surfaced pathway below a caravan site which leads to the road. Turn right down Common Lane, past a terrace of unusual pebble-dashed houses to **BEER** *(shops, services and accommodation; youth hostel; buses to Seaton; car parks; toilets; early closing Thursday).*

More protected from westerlies than anywhere else on Lyme Bay, Beer huddles beneath a weathered chalk cliff, its beach lined with huts and deckchairs. If there is time to spare, a visit to Beer Quarry Caves is recommended. Situated about a mile to the east, the workings are mostly underground. When in production, Beer stone was greatly valued by masons for its working qualities and was used in many notable buildings, among them St. Paul's Cathedral and Westminster Abbey. The complex of great, vaulted chambers bearing many signs of past workmen never fails to impress visitors. There are conducted tours and an informative museum. The caves are open from Easter to end-September, 10.00am. to 6.00pm. 7 days a week. Free parking.

Walk round above a children's playground and past the toilets, staying near the shore to find a tarmac path up the cliffside (Seaton 1¼ miles). A simple 'up and over' walk brings you down steps to a lane where you turn right to **SEATON HOLE** *(summer refreshments;*

The beach at Beer

telephone; toilets). If tide or weather are unfavourable, take the road to Seaton; otherwise turn down right (beach footpath) on a curving track to the shingly beach (dangerous cliffs). About half-way along the row of beach huts stands a seasonal cafe/toilets and the start of a pedestrian promenade leading along into **SEATON** *(all shops, services and accommodation; Tourist Information; buses to Axminster for British Rail connections; car parks; early closing Thursday; electric tramway service during the summer 1½ miles (2.5km) along the old BR Axe Valley line to Colyford.)*

Seaton combines the simply tranquility of small resorts to the west with modern amenities and entertainments; the two do not blend well and result in loss of character. Nevertheless there are numerous places in which to eat, drink and stay overnight and the mile of pebbles provides plenty of space on a sunny day.

SECTION 19 - Seaton to Seatown (Chideock); 13 miles (21km)

An unusual and moderately strenuous walk through a vast overgrown landslip leads out to the picturesque and historic seaside town of Lyme Regis. Recent cliff subsidence has forced an inland detour by road and field path, or a possible low-tide beach walk to Charmouth, famous for its fossils. Over scenic National Trust clifftops, the route ascends steeply to Golden Cap, the south coast's highest point, before dropping over grassy slopes to the little resort of Seatown and nearby Chideock.   Grading - more difficult.

All shops, services and accommodation at Lyme Regis and Charmouth. Shops, refreshments and accommodation at Seatown/Chideock.

NOTE: It is about 7 miles (11km) to Lyme Regis and for much of the way you are walking through the famous Downlands Landslip. The going is convoluted and very hilly; there are no refreshment points and only 1 emergency 'escape route' at about half-way (not a definitive right of way). At other times you are bounded between impenetrable high ground and the sea, though you can walk the shoreline for the last 3 miles (5km). What views there are will be best obtained outside the season of dense foliage, though by the same token the walk is pleasantly shady in hot weather and sheltered from strong winds. The path itself is well walked and maintained throughout by Conservation Corps volunteers, though it can get quite slippery in the wet.

Cross the River Axe road bridge at the east end of Seaton Beach and walk inland for 150m before turning right up a tarmac lane. Keep left of the Axe Cliff Golf Club buildings and continue up a small valley in

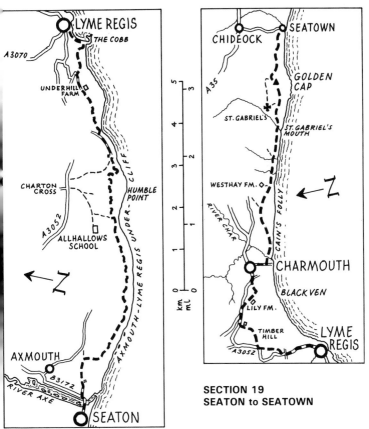

SECTION 19
SEATON to SEATOWN

the golf links (waymarked with white arrows). At the top cross a stile into a farm track. You soon come to a finger post and a notice advising that it will take you 3½ to 4 hours to reach Lyme Regis, that the going can be difficult and that there is no permitted access off the path inland or seawards.

Follow field edges towards the sea, then veer diagonally down across a field, skirting along the clifftops to reach a stile and nature reserve sign - **'AXMOUTH - LYME REGIS UNDERCLIFF.** Established

151

1955-56 by the Nature Conservancy Council'. (For a permit to leave the main pathway, contact the Council at Roughmoor, Bishop's Hull, Taunton.)

Before describing the landslip walk, a few general words of introduction will perhaps enhance an appreciation of this unique environment. The landslip area measures some 5 miles (8km) long by ½ mile (800m) wide and comprises 5 main slippages. The 3 more westerly ones occurred in the early 1800's and 2 of them - Downlands and Whitlands - are well documented owing to the chance presence of the Geological Society's president who was staying at Lyme Regis over Christmas 1839 when the massive subsidence took place.

Rainwater from an excessively wet autumn had permeated the cliff-top layers of porous chalk and greensand which lay on clay tilted about 5 degrees towards the sea. Thus lubricated, some 8 million tons of rock and 20 acres of fields slipped away, forming great chasms, isolated rock masses and even offshore reefs which eventually settled beneath the waves.

Needless to say, the area is of great interest geologically and abounds in fossils. There is equivalent interest in the colonisation by plants and creatures which has developed without man's intervention over a known span of years. Ash woodland is especially common, as is scrub composed of various thorny bushes. A profusion of plant varieties is in evidence and over 100 bird species have been identified, including the nightingale. Mammals include roe deer, foxes, badgers, rabbits and many other rodents: it is outside the scope of this guidebook to mention all the insects, fungi, mosses etc. which thrive in these habitats, but undoubtedly the observant naturalist will gain most from the walk through.

From the signboard, drop down a flight of steps - first of many as the onward path rises, falls and twists. On either side is a continuous and in summer exotic tangle of undergrowth - trees, creepers, ivy and ferns - while up to the left rises the new cliff line.

In due course, Humble Point is visible ahead through the trees and you reach a motorable track from Allhallows School near a tall brick chimney. (The South West Way Association suggest the option of a beach walk from here to Lyme Regis, but progress will inevitably be slower along the foreshore and it should only be attempted at low tide. Good for fossil hunters!)

Turn left up the track and in 20m fork right up a long series of steps. You are roughly half-way but the hardest walking is still to come. At the top, the up and down work intensifies, demanding a steady pace if carrying a heavy pack. At a large tree by a gate you join another track (from the A3052 at Charton Cross) and turn right along it by a water pipe and downhill to a corrugated iron water pumping station. Turn left past the building and walk up the surfaced lane.

At the hilltop the lane drops gently to 2 large trees and a waymark post. Fork right onto a path past the occasional viewpoint and eventually a stile leads out to the access road above Underhill Farm. Turn left up the road and go through a gate on the right opposite a bungalow. At the next handgate keep seaward (aiming towards Portland Bill if it's visible!), where a broad grassy path slants downhill. You have crossed the county border and are now in Dorset.

Suddenly the Cobb is in view below. Fork right at a finger post and beyond the next gate stay along the top of a scrubby copse, turning right over a stile and down steps. In fact, steps lead right down past chalets to the Bowling Club car park where you turn left and walk along the seafront to **LYME REGIS** *(all shops, services and accommodation; Tourist Information; seasonal beach cafes; museum; marine aquarium; buses to Axminister for BR connections; car parks, early closing Thursday).*

Mentioned in the Domesday Book, Lyme Regis was an important Middle Ages sea port - one of Britain's truly 'loyal and ancient boroughs'. Jane Austen often came here (and to neighbouring Charmouth) for her summer holidays and wrote *Persuasion* in a cottage in Broad Street. A nearby bookshop and the old harbour Cobb, which divides the 2 beaches, featured in the film 'The French Lieutenant's Woman'. The pebble beach west of the Cobb was the Duke of Monmouth's landing place in 1685 for his ill-fated attempt to seize the crown of England. History apart, Lyme's colour-washed houses and steep, narrow streets do impart an almost picture-postcard charm. (See the booklet *The Book of the Cobb* by Nigel Clarke available locally.)

NOTE: Several landslips/mudslides have taken away the coast path between Lyme Regis and Charmouth during the past two years. Both the beach and golf course routes are affected, but in fairness to Dorset County Council, they do face great difficulties in establishing a secure path. At low tide only, it should still be possible to take the beach option, providing the big mud slides are avoidable. Otherwise there is a sizeable diversion up round the back of the golf course. (At the time of writing, Dorset County Council intend to make a path line near the clifftop, so watch out for this or enquire at the Tourist Information Office).

Assuming the beach route is unavailable, walk up the A3052 Charmouth road to the top of Dragons Hill (about 1½ miles - 2.5km).

Where the road levels off at a bend, take a path right (east) above the golf course and down through woods to the road. Turn right past a hotel and about 300m after joining the main A25 trunk road, fork off right on a path past Lily Farm which comes out to a lane above Black Ven Nature Reserve west of Charmouth. Turn left then right down the main street *(all shops, services and accommodation; campsite; fossil museum; buses; early closing Thursday)*. A right turn along Lower Sea Lane will take you towards the coast *(summer refreshments)*. **CHARMOUTH** was the home of an amateur geologist, Mary Anning, who unearthed many fossilised reptiles in the landslips and cliffs hereabouts in the early 19th century.

About 200m before the beach, the coast path turns left down a tarmac pathway, crosses the River Char and continues ahead up the wide, firm grassy flanks of Stonebarrow Hill. Rising above the large subsided undercliff of Cain's Folly - a haven for wildlife - you gain superb views back to Lyme Regis and beyond from the 500ft. (150m) level.

Now along the crumbling, orange edge of cliff, you reach a signpost *(left to National Trust Information and car park)*. Still a couple of miles away, Golden Cap interposes itself before the great crescent of Chesil Beach and the wedge of Portland Bill.

Passing a path left for Westhay Farm, keep down the seaward edge of pasture and down over a footbridge. Waymark posts lead on - this is a popular local walk - to cross another substantial bridge (courtesy of the National Trust), whereafter you go straight on up a field above more cliff-falls.

The ascent route ahead is now unequivocal and well signed as you drop first over the final stream above St. Gabriel's Mouth and climb the rather dangerous cliff edge (care needed). A grassy field rises to a fence and stile; steps alleviate the steep, rough summit slopes of **GOLDEN CAP** - 627ft. (191m).

You have climbed to the highest clifftop on the entire Channel coast - as magnificent a viewpoint in all directions as you could wish for, given clear weather: in a gale and rain there is no grimmer a place! The name Golden Cap is said to derive from lighting effects on the yellowish Jurassic limestone. Summit 'furniture' includes a coast path monolith with ammonite imprint and a triangulation pillar.

Steps to the left wind down to a path junction (straight on for St. Gabriel's ruined 13th century church and Tudor farmhouse) where the coast path forks down right over steep grass then on easier ground to **SEATOWN** *(inn, summer cafe in old boathouse; campsite; telephone; small car park)*. 1km inland is **CHIDEOCK** *(shop; pub; accommodation;*

The view east from Golden Cap

buses for Axminster, Bridport and Lyme Regis; early closing Wednesday).

SECTION 20 - Seatown to Abbotsbury; 12 miles (19km)

A stiff climb over 500ft. (155m) cliffs to a small settlement not far from village amenities is followed by a further climb over to the small resort of West Bay, once Bridport's harbour. Clifftop level regained, the going is easier to the vast caravan park at Burton Freshwater and a short river-crossing detour. Picturesque Burton Bradstock lies close by, but the path continues along level cliffs to Burton Beach and the start of the great pebble ridge known as Chesil Bank. Soon at sea level, you skirt marshy lakes on

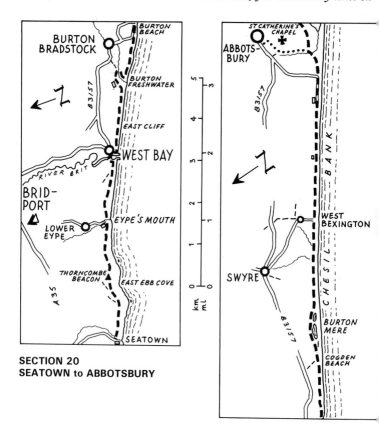

SECTION 20
SEATOWN to ABBOTSBURY

awkward shingle to West Bexington (where an inland variant links with Osmington Mills beyond Weymouth). On a rough track beside Chesil Bank you reach the ancient village of Abbotsbury, with its famous Swannery, sub-tropical gardens and old buildings. Grading - more difficult to West Bay, then moderate, becoming easy.

Refreshments and accommodation off-route at Lower Eype. Shops, services and accommodation (mostly seasonal) at West Bay. Seasonal camp shops at Burton Freshwater. Pubs off-route at Burton Bradstock. Summer refreshments at Burton Beach. Refreshments and accommodation at West Bexington (youth hostel 3 miles - 5km - inland at Little Cheney).

Leaving Seatown, the coast path climbs Ridge Cliff steeply to Doghouse Hill summit above East Ebb Cove and undulates over to Thorncombe Beacon, with its wartime pillbox - a considerable ascent to 509ft. (155m) from sea level. Still above subsided cliffs (though virtually the last for a while) you drop through a small valley and continue down the steep cliff edge to the buildings at **EYPE'S MOUTH** *(car park; campsite. Pub, accommodation and Post Office 600m inland at Lower Eype).*

Steps and stepping stones from the road-end cross the little stream, then there is a straightforward climb over West Cliff outside field boundaries, ending past holiday homes and sea defences down at the western end of the promenade at **WEST BAY** *(shops, services and accommodation; youth hostel in Bridport - buses; International Holiday Centre; campsite; car parking; toilets; early closing Thursday).*

Before the railway came in 1884, West Bay was Bridport's harbour. Bridport itself, a busy market town, is noted for its rope and net making (hence the wide streets) - products which were exported as early as the 1300's. Rather exposed and prone to silting up, this harbour at the mouth of the River Brit is used by pleasure craft and a small fishing fleet. Unfortunately, one cannot say that resort development at West Bay has been tastefully carried out! As recently as 1974, the town was inundated by gale-lashed waves and suffered much damage. Considerable sums have been spent strengthening its sea defences, which were completed - for the time being - in 1984.

Walk round the harbour basin and back to the shore. The shingle beach shelves steeply and bathing is dangerous - a characteristic of the shoreline all the way to Weymouth. At the east end of the beach, go through a fence gap (signed Bexington 6 miles) and climb the steep grassy cliff edge onto East Cliff. Level walking outside a golf course follows, with very good views of Chesil Bank ahead.

Beyond a small valley, the coast path drops to the beach (keep to the

On the cliffs between West Bay and Burton Freshwater

right-hand trod) at **BURTON FRESHWATER.** Unsightly caravans on the beach spill over from the large site *(food store, newsagent, launderette, toilets, amusements - all seasonal)*. Pass a coast path sign and walk along the beach, turning left on a small inland detour along the top of a grassy embankment. (If the River Bride is very low, it might be possible to wade the shingle channel, but great discretion is called for when assessing the depth and strength of current.)

Where the embankment ends by some camp toilets, turn right along the campsite loop track (south-east) towards a finger post in a hedged bank at the far end of the field. Go through a gap and over the footbridge, veering right towards the coast. *(Burton Bradstock lies just ½ mile to the left - an exceptionally picturesque Dorset village, with an old flax mill, church and 3 pubs - there used to be 14!)*

At the cliff edge, turn up left outside a fence; pleasant walking leads easily to a tarmac lane but the inner trod is preferable to the precarious seaward one. Keep ahead parallel to the lane past a hotel *(bar/restaurant)*, down to **BURTON BEACH** *(summer refreshments; car park)*.

Opinions seem to differ over the location of **CHESIL BANK'S** western extremity. Vestiges of this great, curving pebble ridge exist as far west as Eype's Mouth, but its true identity is dissipated beyond Burton Cliff. It is an extraordinary topographical feature, distinctive

On the Chesil Bank near West Bexington

even on small-scale maps and, apart from minor versions such as Loe Bar in Mount's Bay, a unique land form on the south coast.

The Chesil (Anglo-Saxon for 'stones') extends 18 miles (29km) in a gentle south-east to north-west arc from Portland. Its pebbles are graded in size by west-to-east currents, from large 3″ cobbles at Portland to fine pea-gravel in the west (though it is not known why other pebble banks lack this progression). It is claimed that local fishermen landing in fog or darkness could determine their exact position by the size of the pebbles!

Continuing along low cliffs, you reach a car park at Cogden Beach and come inland a little to pass the marshy lakes of Burton Mere. Once much larger, these drained and cultivated reed beds are being gradually smothered by encroaching pebbles.

It is uncomfortable walking on loose shingle to the seafront car park at **WEST BEXINGTON** *(cafe; toilets. Pub, hotels, Post Office and telephone 500m up lane in village. Youth hostel at Litton Cheney, 3 miles (5km) inland).*

NOTE: From here to Osmington Mills beyond Weymouth, there is an inland alternative to the coastal route. It is about 7 miles (11km) shorter than the coast path and follows elevated ground via the Hardy Monument and the Dorset Ridgeway. Excellent views are obtained, both inland and coastal, and the path passes many sites of archaeo-

159

logical interest.

Like the author, dedicated coastal walkers may not feel inclined to deviate so far from the shoreline, thus missing the essential flavour of the east Fleet, Weymouth and the cliffs beyond. However, the following brief summary is provided for those attracted to this high level option. For detailed path notes, consult the South West Way Association's annual handbook.

INLAND VARIANT ON THE DORSET RIDGEWAY
From WEST BEXINGTON to OSMINGTON MILLS

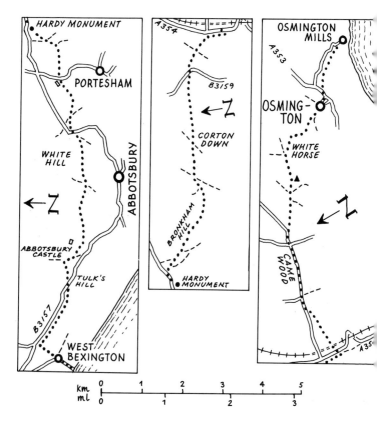

Follow the road inland to West Bexington and continue straight ahead towards the B3517 road, walking below it to Tulk's Hill which is crossed to reach Abbotsbury Castle Hill Fort. Passing Wears Hill Farm, you keep east along fields for a mile over White Hill, staying parallel to a small wood on the left and crossing a farm road. Continue eastwards over the Portesham road and follow signs up through woods to Hardy Monument.

The way now veers south-east along Bronkham Hill to Corton Down then east again, passing numerous tumuli and within sight of the Maiden Castle earthwork to the north. From the A354 you reach a minor road past Came Wood, leading to a path along above Osmington White Horse. Dropping south-east to Osmington village, a short stretch on the A353 and a right turn lead down to Osmington Mills.

Pub, shop, Post Office and accommodation off-route at Portesham. Cafe, pub, Post Office accommodation and buses to Weymouth at Osmington (early closing Wednesday).

Proceeding east from West Bexington Beach - popular with sea anglers and bird watchers - the coast path takes to a rough track behind The Chesil which here is no more than a low, gentle slope of fine shingle. Adjacent low-lying fields get waterlogged in winter. Rising imperceptibly you pass old Coastguard cottages and a few hauled-up boats and then the track (Smugglers Walk) is surfaced all the way to Abbotsbury.

To seaward, the occasional subsided wartime blockhouse, upturned boat or sea fisherman are the only interruptions in the vastness of the pebble bank which seems to stretch into infinity. It is theoretically feasible to trudge the remaining 9 miles (14km) to Portland and thus stay close to the sea. However, the going can be extremely arduous and your walking pace reduced to half by the energy absorbtion of displaced pebbles at each footfall. In many ways it is a wilderness walk - few plants survive on the storm-lashed pebble ridge, though above the high water mark are the stout sea-kale, the purple flowered sea-pea and sea-campion. In summer there are splashes of colour here and there - thrift, ragwort, yellow poppies and cranesbill - especially on the lee side.

NOTE: East of Abbotsbury, the bank is separated from the mainland by a brackish tidal lagoon known as The Fleet and dotted with both resident and migrant bird species. The Chesil Bank opposite The Fleet - right along to Portland - is closed to visitors from 1st May to 31st August for the Schedule 1 bird nesting season. Throughout the rest of the year, access is permitted along the seaward flanks of the bank only. For possible dispensation, contact the Warden of Strangeways Estate.

Abbotsbury

A final word of caution: if intending to set out along Chesil Bank, allow twice the normal walking time, carry energy rations and obtain a weather forecast. The bank is no place to be in a storm - large ships have been carried right over the crest by waves and there is, of course, no shelter. The walker's only escape is to retrace steps or carry on - whichever is the shorter distance!

Arriving at **ABBOTSBURY** car park *(toilets)*, you are a mile from the village itself *(shops; pub; some accommodation; Post Office; telephone; toilets; buses; early closing Thursday)*. Abbotsbury is well worth exploring if time allows. There are sub-tropical gardens (open mid-March to October daily), the famous 400 year-old Swannery (open mid-May to mid-September daily), a fine 15th century tithe barn, old cottages and hilltop St. Catherine's Chapel.

The coast path continues on a track to seaward of the car park and goes through a handgate at signs for the Swannery and into a green lane. Where this swings inland alongside a stream, turn right over a stile (signed 'coast path and Swannery'). (To detour through Abbotsbury, continue up inland, fork right through a gate by a white footpath sign and walk up by an ivy-clad wall. Fork left (right to St. Catherine's Chapel) into the village. Here turn right and take the next road off right past the abbey ruins and down to barns at an acute bend to rejoin the main coast path route - see below.)

From the stile, you climb round the base of Chapel Hill, once used to spot mackerel shoals, and pass a stone slab sign. Continue over the footbridge, walking left inland on the Swannery track to the road and turning right, down to the acute bend by barns on the outskirts of Abbotsbury.

SECTION 21 - Abbotsbury to Weymouth;   14 miles (23km)

A hilly inland detour offering wide coastal views at first leads through fields back to the shoreline of The Fleet. Bird life is of special interest as you skirt one of Britain's oldest nature reserves on a flat, field-edge path to East Fleet hamlet. With the option of public transport to Weymouth from nearby Chickerell or Charlestown a little farther on, you pass a firing range and

Swans on The Fleet

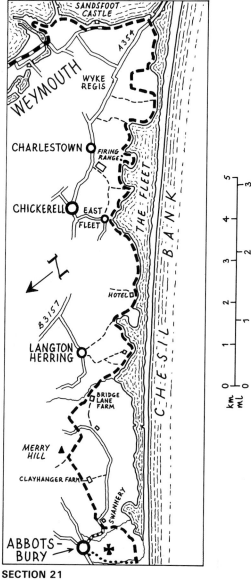

SANDSFOOT
CASTLE

A 354

WEYMOUTH

WYKE
REGIS

CHARLESTOWN — FIRING
RANGE

CHICKERELL — EAST
FLEET

T H E   F L E E T

C H E S I L   B A N K

HOTEL

B 3157

LANGTON
HERRING

BRIDGE
LANE
FARM

MERRY
HILL

CLAYHANGER FARM

SWANNERY

ABBOTS-
BURY

km.
ml.

0   1   2   3   4   5
0   1   2   3

SECTION 21
ABBOTSBURY to WEYMOUTH

holiday caravans on the approach to the main road causeway to the Isle of Portland. Along by Portland Harbour, road and paths take you through gardens to the harbour quaysides in central Weymout. Grading - moderate, becoming easy.

Summer teas at Clayhanger Farm. Pub/restaurant and Post Office off-route at Langton Herring. Meals and accommodation at Manor House Hotel. Shop, cafe, Post Office, accommodation and buses at Chickerell, similar at Charlestown. Pub and summer refreshments at the A354 Portland causeway.

Although it is possible to walk along Chesil Bank (see Section 20), this is unlikely to attract many walkers, the majority of whom will wish to continue on the official coast path which now makes a rather agricultural detour inland, by-passing the first half of The Fleet. Walk notes now resume by barns at the acute bend in the B road (New Barn Road) just north of the Swannery.

At a finger post, turn left by barns and you will quickly come round to cross a stile. Aim half-right to a wall corner, then walk up a groove on the left, thereafter keeping uphill through grassy hollows and up the crest of Linton Hill (the route once went along New Barns Road below). Extensive views open out as you gain height and the next mile or so provides exhilarating walking along a small escarpment.

You pass Clayhanger Farm *(summer teas, 3.00pm. to 6.00pm)* and after several stiles arrive at a green track and signpost just short of Merry Hill. From here onwards, there is little evidence of a path on the ground. Turn down right, through a small thicket and down the edge of a small wood. At its bottom corner, pass through 2 handgates, turn left and walk along to meet New Barn Road again, crossing it and going eastwards up the field ahead. At the top go through a hedge gap on the left, then right at a coast path sign, aiming for the top left edge of Wyke Wood.

Follow the wood downhill - if visibility allows, the onward route eventually reaches cottages on the distant hillside above The Fleet. Turn left along by a stream in a narrow field to a stile just east of **BRIDGE LANE FARM** then aim for another stile at the seaward end of the large field: from here the next post should be visible in a hedge where the path crosses a stream.

You are now walking down a shallow, grassy and wooded stream valley. Appoaching The Fleet, you pass a path left up to Langton Herring *(16th century pub/restaurant; Post Office)* and swing right along and up a field edge above an inlet. The way crosses a lane from the cottages opposite a small boathouse on Chesil Bank and proceeds along more field edges to a footbridge and stile (track left to Langton

Chesil Bank from above Fortuneswell

Herring). Turn right along by a wall across the Herbury promontory (Weymout 8 miles).

It is best to walk along the little beach at Gore Cove, then left up through a thicket and past the Manor House Hotel *(meals and accommodation)* associated (as the Moonfleet Hotel) with the 18th century smuggling story *Moonfleet* by J.M.Faulkner. Head down towards the shore, through a copse and back up to the shoreline path which continues straightforwardly along field boundaries.

With such easy walking, there is time to look around at this unusual environment. The Fleet Sanctuary is Britain's 2nd oldest nature reserve, whose origins date back to 1393 when the protection of mute swans was initiated: swans - mostly from Abbotsbury - are still very much in evidence. Preventing any development on Chesil Bank, the Sanctuary contains a range of different habitats and has been recognised as an internationally important wetland. In its protected shallows live many unusual marine plants and animals and fish come here to spawn. The bank itself is home for rare seabirds and shingle flowers.

At The Fleet's widest point, you approach **EAST FLEET**. A row of cottages and the remains of a tiny old church are all that survived the great storm of 1824 which wreaked havoc all along this coast. Don't go up to the buildings (unless to look!) but carry on round the shoreline. *(If, however, you wish to catch a bus for the 3 miles (5km) to Weymouth, Chickerell is only 800m inland; it has a shop, cafe, pub, Post Office and accommodation.)*

Within a mile, the coast path reaches Chickerell Camp and the firing range at **CHARLESTOWN.** When the red flags are flying, firing is in progress and you divert across the headland, at other times walking round it. A track inland takes you to the B3157 at Charlestown and another opportunity to catch a bus into Weymouth. Indeed, because the onward coast path deteriorates considerably in quality from here on, many walkers take the public transport option to make better use of their time exploring Weymouth.

For those continuing along The Fleet, you pass a caravan park at the back of Linch Cove and go up round a field boundary. Watch for a recent diversion inland at Wyke Regis to by-pass a Service establishment before passing more caravans and reaching the A354 at the holiday park entrance *(summer refreshments and toilets at nearby car park)*.

The Fleet is quite deep here and seawater seepage maintains more salinity than farther west. Traditional 'lerrets' - local 4 or 6 oared boats, pointed at bow and stern - were first recorded in the 1600's but have disappeared in recent years (a good example can be found in Weymouth museum). They will not be found amongst the many moored boats or the rotting hulls along the bank. At this Portland end, the Chesil stands an impressive 30ft. (9m) high, falling in two steep shelves to the sea; its stones are too large to retain humus and nutrients for plant life. Walking to the bank's summit where the air is filled with the hypnotic growl of waves on pebbles, one can gaze westwards - perhaps in awe - at the vastness of this natural phenomenon.

Cross the busy main road *(buses for Weymouth)* opposite the Royal Victoria pub - the coast path eschews a circuit of Portland Bill - where a path on the line of a dismantled railway leads along the shore of Portland Harbour with its warships lying at anchor inside the great offshore breakwaters.

A road takes you past the ruins of Sandsfoot Castle, built in 1539 as part of Henry VIII's south coast harbour defences, and in a further 400m you can turn right on leafy Undercliff Walk, emerging at Nothe Gardens above the harbour. Either cross on the little summer ferry or walk to the Town Bridge near the centre of **WEYMOUTH** *(all shops, services and accommodation; British Rail station; coach station and buses; museum; etc. early closing Wednesday)*.

Very much a seaside resort with a magnificent sandy beach and all the usual amenities, Weymouth town has few buildings of historical interest other than bow-windowed houses and old pubs around the harbour quaysides and a few town centre alleys. However this was a fashionable watering hole and was much patronised towards the end of the 18th century by George III, who would enter the waves in his bathing machine while his musicians played 'God Save the King'! His colourful statue stands right on the seafront. Thomas Hardy used Weymouth - re-named Budmouth - in many of his novels. For a fascinating insight into Weymouth's history and development, visit the museum at Westham Road by the bridge (open daily except winter Sundays).

NOTE: Long-distance walkers travelling east would do well to check whether the Lulworth to Kimmeridge Range Walk coast path is open at their expected time of arrival. For details please see Section 22.

Statue of George III, Weymouth seafront

SECTION 22 - Weymouth to Lulworth Cove; 11 miles (18km)

Beyond Weymouth's long seafront, the coast path reaches a popular little cove before crossing open cliffs, passing a holiday camp and traversing rougher terrain to the old pub at Osmington Mills hamlet. Gentle clifftops lead on past the site of a medieval village, whereafter you climb to the first of many lofty chalk cliffs. On steeper and more sustained gradients, the way dips and climbs past the famous Durdle Door beauty spot, easing on the final well walked path over to Lulworth Cove. Grading - moderate, but strenuous between White Nothe and Durdle Door.

Refreshments and nearby accommodation at Overcombe. Hotel and holiday camp amenities at Bowleaze Cove. Refreshments, accommodation, campsite and nearby shop at Osmington Mills.

Walking the entire length of Weymouth's 2 mile (3km) seafront is not to everyone's liking and if time presses you can catch a bus to Overcombe Corner where the road finally swings inland. The promenade as such ends half-way along, but you can continue atop the sea wall.

At **OVERCOMBE** *(cafe; Post Office; nearby pub and accommodation; buses; toilets)*, the official coast path takes to the minor road up from a garage near the toilets and crosses grass down to **BOWLEAZE COVE** at the mouth of the River Jordan *(bar/restaurant, shop, amusements, etc. at the holiday camp; nearby hotel)*. On the way over Furzy Cliff you will have passed near the foundations of a small Roman temple on Jordan Hill.

(From Overcombe cafe, it might be possible to walk on along the sea wall. The low, clayey cliff is stabilised with stone facing for 150m but is prone to subsidence beyond. At the time of writing you can easily cross the slipped area and continue to Bowleaze Cove. At low tide the shingly beach is another - more tiring - option.)

Proceed to seaward of the hotel and out onto open downland, the path broad and straightforward. Over to the north from Redcliff Point you will see the figure of George III on his horse, cut from the chalk above Sutton Poynz.

Soon the way passes outside the perimeter fence at Shortlake House holiday camp and turns right (about 72 degrees if in mist!) at a stile up across rough grassy slopes to a hilltop finger post (don't follow the coast itself). Keep straight ahead towards a large thicket, with views ahead of White Nothe, the first in a long series of magnificent chalk cliffs. You enter the thicket through gorse, brambles and nettles, cross 2 stiles and continue along above undergrowth on a low field ridge to the next post.

169

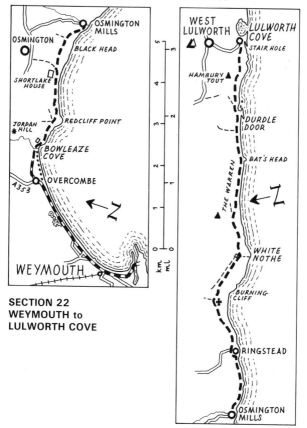

**SECTION 22
WEYMOUTH to
LULWORTH COVE**

Past ancient earthworks, **BLACK HEAD** is reached - rather a 'non-headland' - and you go down through a marshy valley on timber planks. Emerging, turn right and the path slants up in a wide swath from the sloping cliff edge. Topping a rise, Osmington Mills appears below. Keep round towards the sea and down past bushes, through a tunnel of undergrowth and down recently installed timber steps on a landslip-prone slope to reach a large car park *(toilets; display boards about Portland)*. Head directly down to the 15th century Smugglers Inn *(meals, snacks, drinks, teas)* at **OSMINGTON MILLS** *(also accommodation; camping; supermarket; telephone - about 800m up road.*

Osmington village has a shop, cafe, pub, Post Office, accommodation and buses but is a mile inland; early closing Wednesday).

Turn left round the side of the Smugglers Inn and pick up a surfaced footpath leading past houses and out to the cliffs, climbing back to the edge through bushes. Good views are obtained back to Weymouth and Portland Bill. Descending gently over grass, you pass 2 red brick wartime pillboxes 500m apart - both unfortunately rendered useless to the walker by cattle - continuing between bushes along to **RINGSTEAD** *(summer refreshments; hotel; car park; toilets)*. All that remains of this medieval village are mounds and hollows just south of Glebe Cottage; it was probably depopulated by the black death or pirate raids.

The official path takes you inland here, not along the seafront as you would expect. A wide track to the right of the road passes bungalows and climbs gently through a wood to emerge on the slopes of Burning Cliff (named after the spontaneous combustion of oil shale in 1826 which burned for over a year). Keep to the cliff edge path above a National Trust landslip area and nature reserve, crossing a stile adjacent to a chapel and rising to a fence by old Coastguard cottages on **WHITE NOTHE** (548ft. - 167m). Be careful here to take the left fork - the right one drops abruptly to the undercliff - very slippery in wet weather.

From this point eastwards stretches a succession of chalk cliffs where the rolling downs meet the sea. Between here and Swanage, walkers are promised some of the most dramatically beautiful coastal scenery on the entire South West Way - some of the toughest gradients too! Cliff formations and contorted rock strata provide continuing interest, even for those unacquainted with geology, while bird life, wild flowers, springy turf and superlative views each add their own increment of pleasure to the walking. Such rewards, however, are not gained without effort and the ensuing 4 miles (6km) to Lulworth Cove provide a foretaste of what is to come!

Veering slightly inland round the back of a small combe, you pass a navigation beacon on the left (a second beacon is out of sight) and cross down through The Warren - an ancient Celtic field system - on the first of many 'big-dipper' descents. The small promontory of Bat's Head shows vertical chalk and flint strata as you climb over its neck to Swyre Head.

The natural rock arch at **DURDLE DOOR** must be one of Britain's most photographed coastal features. Over the years it has become an extremely popular beauty spot, with the clear waters of Man o' War and Durdle Door beaches attracting snorkellers and bathers. Adding

171

St. Oswald's Bay from above Durdle Door

to hordes of day trippers walking over from Lulworth Cove is the population of a camping and caravan site partly concealed in woods above the bay. So for a mile or so you will have company on the path, in summer at least, though few visitors venture farther away from the nearest car park than this!

The clear path climbs easier slopes above St. Oswald's Bay and Dungy Head, affording good retrospective views of the humpy cliffs. A broad chalky pathway - a veritable walker's motorway - drops fairly steeply across the flanks of Hambury Tout to the vast car park *(turn left at stile for the youth hostel)* at **LULWORTH COVE** *(cafes; restaurants; pub; accommodation; Post Office; telephone; gift shops; Information Centre; buses; toilets; early closing Saturday).*

Rather overrun by tourists in the summer months, Lulworth Cove is nevertheless an interesting spot and provides a welcome opportunity for walkers to break their journey on this long and relatively lonely stretch of strenuous going. The old village, renowned for its smuggling exploits in the early 1700's, lies up inland, but tourist development has extended it seawards.

If you walk up from the car park's southern corner and cross a small road, you can climb to the famous Stair Hole, a collapsed sea cave with spectacular cliff folding and arches. Down at Lulworth Cove Beach,

Lulworth Cove

much patronised by divers and boat owners, the circular cove's geological formation can be appreciated: having breached a band of harder Portland limestone along the outer cliff line, the sea has worn back softer rocks with remarkable symmetry.

SECTION 23 - Lulworth Cove to Worth Matravers;   12 miles (19km)

One of the great coastal walking experiences on the South West Way awaits you between Lulworth Cove and Gaulter Gap. Much of this initial 7 miles (11km) lies within the Lulworth Gunnery Ranges and walkers are advised to verify that these are open to the public before setting off (details below). Some long and fierce gradients, with no refreshment points along the way, make this section unsuitable for all but the moderately fit and the going can be harder still in rough weather. Exhilarating but strenuous walking takes you past an extensive Iron Age hill fort and through the derelict Ranges village of Tyneham, finally descending more gently to Kimmeridge Bay. Leaving the Ranges behind, you pass an oil well, a folly tower and continue along clifftops above the Kimmeridge Ledges. Another major ascent leads to a recent landslip diversion inland, a short distance from the village of Worth Matravers. Grading - strenuous to Gaulter Gap, then more difficult. Ice-creams in summer at Gaulter Gap. Meals, drinks and Post Office/stores 1 mile off-route at Kimmeridge.

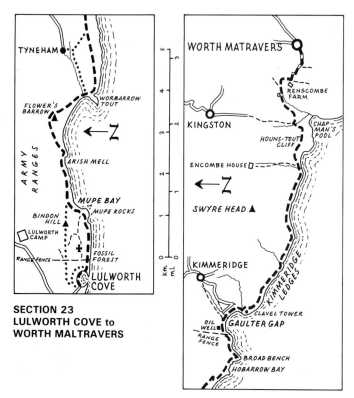

**SECTION 23
LULWORTH COVE to
WORTH MALTRAVERS**

NOTE: In 1974, following the report of the Defence Lands Committee chaired by Lord Nugent, the government agreed to increase public access to the 7,000 acres of land east of Lulworth, used for many years as army firing ranges. The Lulworth Range Walks, including the coast path itself, were thus instigated.

They are normally open to the public every Saturday and Sunday, except for about 6 weekends a year which are reserved by the Royal Armoured Corps Gunnery School for firing practice. Additionally, the Range Walks are opened up during traditional holiday periods - ie. Christmas, Easter, Spring Bank Holiday, Whitsun and from the end of July to the beginning of September.

Since the alternative to the Range Walk coast path is a tiresome 12 mile (19km) road bash from West Lulworth to Kimmeridge via East Lulworth (or hitch-hiking or taxi), walkers are strongly urged to check whether the coast path is open well in advance of arrival in the area. This information is available from various sources:-

a)   The Range Officer, R.A.C. Gunnery School, Lulworth, Dorset, Tel: Bindon Abbey (0929) 462721 ext. 819 (office hours Monday to Friday and during firing weekends).

b)   The Guardroom, Tel: Bindon Abbey (0929) 462721 ext. 824 (anytime).

c)   The local press.

d)   The South West Way Association's annual handbook.

Some 70,000 shells are fired on the ranges each year and inevitably a few ricochet off target or fail to explode. Before the Range Walks are opened, they are searched for unexploded shells, but this process cannot guarantee safety for walkers who stray from the paths. A common sense safey code asks walkers to remain on paths waymarked with yellow-tipped posts, to comply with any instructions from wardens, not to pick up ammunition or use metal detectors, to keep away from all buildings (except at Tyneham), not to camp or light fires, to beware dangerous cliffs and to refrain from collecting wildlife or fossil specimens without permission.

Already an area of outstanding beauty, the ranges have been protected for decades from the hand of man. Consequently much has been preserved that would otherwise have disappeared beneath the plough, chemical spray or bulldozer. Grasslands are 'unimproved', herbicides, pesticides and pollution unknown, so that habitats support an exceptional variety of flora and fauna: even the birds have grown accumstomed to the firing!

Ancient earthworks and medieval field systems have survived, while features of more recent, pre-war agricultural practice have been left to revert to natural development. Whatever your views on the Armed Forces' justification for occupying this and other stretches of Britain's countryside, their claim to have protected the Lulworth Ranges area from the negative aspects of human exploitation does seem well founded.

The coast path between the Range gates at Fossil Forest and Kimmeridge is 6½ miles (10.5km) in length, with no refreshment or accommodation points, and is graded 'strenuous'. In rough weather particularly, be prepared for an energetic few hours!

From Lulworth Cove there are 2 main options to reach Bindon Hill

175

above Mupe Bay, assuming the Ranges are open: a high level route with wide views most of the way and the coast path route near the Fossil Forest and round by Mupe Rocks.

High level route: From just above the slipway beach shop at Lulworth Cove, go up steps left past a private swimming pool and over a stile (left to youth hostel). More steps lead up, climbing back left on a chalky path to mount the ridge of Radar Hill. It is a sheepy ascent, the path petering out as you approach the radar station and West Lulworth Gate in the Ranges fence.

Go through the fence handgate and along a track, over the radar station's access road, forking left along **BINDON HILL'S** chalk trackway. At the summit are a navigation light, a flagpole and a stone pillar dedicated to R.A.C. soldiers whose ashes are scattered in the area. Continue eastwards between yellow-tipped posts (which will become very familiar) to a post where the coastal route joins.

Coast path route: Provided the tide is low enough you can walk along the shingle/pebble beach below Lulworth Cove's high cliffs. At the far end either turn left up steps then right at a finger post across an overgrown stream bed and onto Peppler Point; or if the tide is in, leave the road above the cove and take the path rising 300ft. (91m) along the clifftops, dropping to the same point.

Turn east along the shoreline and watch for the well known Fossil Forest below on a rock ledge (access steps down right). Even from above there is a good view of fossilised tree stumps dating back 200 million years to the age of the dinosaurs. Just inland is the site of Bindon Abbey, the present privately owned building of 13th century origin.

At a white flagpole you pass through the Ranges gate and walk on above more fossil remains. With the long ridge of Bindon Hill to landward, you cross the access track to a radar installation and come round by a concrete bunker above Mupe Rocks. Ahead are the big earthworks on Flower's Barrow, the jagged profile of Gad Cliff and distant St. Aldhelm's Head. Delightful walking follows over unspoiled grassland dotted with gorse above **MUPE BAY** *(steep steps to beach - bathing allowed)*.

At a gravel track and finger post for Kimmeridge, you engage the formidable climb up Bindon Hill and from a stile onwards, the legwork really begins. At first by a wire fence (useful hand holds!), the chalky path veers away right. Near the top a new zig-zag avoids dangerous ground but you are still poised above a precipitous and substantial drop. Views are tremendous, taking in Portland Bill and Weymouth to the west, Poole Harbour and Bournemouth to the east,

St.Aldhelm's Head (distant top) from Gad Cliff

and the 17th century Lulworth Castle 2 miles inland.

Reaching the post on Cockpit Head where the high level option joins, you turn right, dipping towards a narrow ridge then descending very steeply to **ARISH MELL** *(beach closed to public - outlet for Winfrith Nuclear Research Station 4½ miles (7km) to the north-west).*

The next long pull up takes you away from the coastal edge to **FLOWER'S BARROW,** an important Iron Age hill fort on Ring's Hill (568ft. - 173m). Covering 15½ acres, its enclosures, banks, ditches, occupation platforms and entrance are all discernible, though it seems likely that as much as a third of the original site fell away prior to the 18th century. Also on this lofty summit, you join the old Dorset Coastal Ridgeway which heads inland to Lowford Sheard, Whitway and thence now by road to Kimmeridge.

Steep and very slippery in wet weather, the big descent to Worbarrow Bay almost reaches sea level at **WORBARROW TOUT** ('Tout' being Old English for lookout). On the way down there are views across to Tyneham village. Above the beach stands a viewing tablet bearing an artist's impression of how the little complex of estate buildings - boathouse, cottage, lifeboat house - appeared in pre-army days: all that remains today are foundations and a few low walls.

The coast path now rises up the steep shoulder of **GAD CLIFF,** easing off along the top, but a detour to visit Tyneham is highly recommended. You can rejoin the coast path further along Gad Cliff, adding nothing to the mileage.

TYNEHAM appears in the Domesday Book and was a small rural

Gad Cliff from the ranges path

community up to World War II. It is surrounded by signs of Iron Age and medieval settlement, most significantly extensive ancient field systems. The fact that so much has been left intact is due to a considerable irony, for the village itself is derelict. The Tyneham valley was adopted as a firing range by the army in 1943 and its inhabitants re-housed on the understanding they could return at the end of the war. This promise was never honoured and the 'ghost village' has been unoccupied ever since.

When the Ranges are open, the village is much visited by motorists who drive down from West Creech Hill. To cater for increasing public interest, permanent exhibitions have been installed by the Heritage Coast team in the church and the schoolroom, explaining the history and development of the Ranges environment (open 10.00am. to 4.00pm.). There are no facilities here *(other than the car park and toilets)* but a good deal to interest the visitor, given a modicum of imagination. It also makes a fine picnic spot in good weather.

To reach Tyneham from Worbarrow Tout, simply walk up the motorable track (about 20 minutes). To rejoin the coast path, walk back past the toilets and take a path signed 'Tyneham Cap' which climbs the steep hillside to Gad Cliff. There are breathtaking views forward from this high vantage point where cliff edge subsidence has

The 'Nodding Donkey' oil well at Kimmeridge Bay

opened up viewpoints, not only to St. Aldhelm's Head but vertically down to dark rock reefs in turquoise shallows.

Reaching a sign, you fork right over a stile *(straight on over Tyneham Cap on the Ridgeway leads to Kimmeridge village - meals, drinks, Post Office/stores)*, angling down over grass and following the ubiquitous posts. The path zig-zags back then drops down easy slopes above **HOBARROW BAY,** with the amazing low tide rock platforms on Broad Bank seen to good effect. Also on the descent, glance back to the extraordinary multiple buttresses on Gad Cliff, invisible until now.

The well cleared and flowery track winds gently down towards Kimmeridge Bay and leaves the Ranges at Kimmeridge Gate. Almost immediately you pass an oil well! The dark brown bituminous shale found here was once burned as fuel and called Kimmeridge Coal, though it never proved commercially viable owing to the emission of sulphurous fumes.

Prospecting for oil began in 1936 but it was 1961 before production started. Owned by BP, the green-painted, electric-powered 'nodding donkey' is a great favourite with school field trips. The oil is taken by road and rail to the Llandarcy Refinery in South Wales. Much greater

The Clavel Tower from Kimmeridge Bay

oil reserves have been discovered elsewhere in Dorset, notably at Wytch Farm and adjacent fields. It is estimated that the county's total oil reserves would serve Britain's needs for about 10 months.

150m along the access road, fork right on a path past old cottages, over a stream and up across a grassy car park *(summer ice-creams)* at **GAULTER GAP,** part of the private Smedmore Estate *(licensed restaurant, coffees, teas and snacks all at the Post Ofice/stores in* **KIMMERIDGE,** *a mile up the toll road or on field paths).*

With Worth Matravers now about 5 miles (8km) ahead, the coast path keeps seaward over another car park and turns right by toilets down a lane to the cove, popular with divers. Kimmeridge's rocky shore is especially rich in marine life which thrives in the large area of shallow water extending a mile offshore.

Turn left up steps through trees and up to the **CLAVEL TOWER,** a ruined folly (or possibly observatory) built in 1820 by the Rev. John Clavel of Smedmore and later used as a Coastguard lookout.

Along field edges, the path undulates above the seaweed-covered Kimmeridge Ledges, crosses a footbridge and climbs over a spur coming down from Swyre Head. From the waterfall at the valley leading up to Encombe House, it has been possible at very low tides to descend steps and walk along the beach to Chapman's Pool, but both steps and waterfall were impassable at the author's last visit. Chances are you will have to climb the 500ft. (140m) to **HOUNS-TOUT CLIFF**, involving a substantial effort!

Passing a track left to Kingston *(inn; Post Office)* at the top, you descend steps and watch for a recent diversion (well signed) inland at a higher level than the old path which traversed the extremely unstable undercliff above **CHAPMAN'S POOL**. The way bears inland at a field gate by a cattle-grid and 'Beach Closed' sign, and is way-marked seawards again from the houses (Hillbottom).

To finish this section, follow the surfaced track over the stream, climbing east up a small valley and swinging right up to 17th century Renscombe Farm *(car parking)*. Now simply walk about 1km along to the picturesque village of **WORTH MATRAVERS** *(inn; seasonal cafe; some accommodation; Field Studies Centre; Post Office; infrequent buses; car park)*, with its fine Norman church and quaint old cottages.

The environs of Worth Matravers is steeped in history, from Bronze Age occupation to the Domesday survey of 1086. Westminster Abbey, Salisbury Cathedral and many public buildings in London incorporate local stone - either the so-called 'Purbeck Marble' or sea-cliff Purbeck Limestone - which has been quarried from the area since Roman times. Wild flowers, butterflies and seabirds abound on the open downland and steep cliffs.

SECTION 24 - Worth Matravers to Poole Harbour;   16 miles (26km)

Unstable undercliff and a steep climb lead to the Norman chapel and Coast-guard lookout on St. Aldhelm's Head, after which you pass a succession of disused quarries on high limestone cliffs (less steep than the previous section). Although open and remote from habitation, a good network of paths link the coast to inland villages. Beyond the lighthouse on Anvil Point you enter a country park where well walked tracks past many features of interest bring you to the family resort of Swanage. An ascent onto Ballard Down is followed by easy walking to the famous Old Harry Rocks and a gentle descent to Studland village. A long sandy bay concludes this section (and the South West Way for eastbound walkers) at South Haven Point, whence a frequent ferry runs across to Poole and Bournemouth.   Grading - more difficult to Durlston Head, then easy except for the stiff climb to Ballard Down.

Refreshments at Durlston Castle. All shops, services and accommodation, including youth hostel, at Swanage. Refreshments, shop and accommodation at Studland.

To regain the coast path, walk back to Renscombe Farm, turn left on a stony track and just beyond the little car park, take a footpath on the right for 400m; this links up to the coast path on West hill clifftop above Chapman's Pool.

Running alongside dry-stone walls, with wonderful views past Kimmeridge and White Nothe to Portland Bill, the way crosses Emmett's Hill and drops steeply through a valley (Pier Bottom) below a working quarry. It then mounts a long flight of steps, passes a memorial seat and reaches **ST. ALDHELM'S** (or locally, **ST. ALBAN'S) HEAD** - 350ft. (107m) above the sea.

The squat, square Norman chapel with walls a metre thick is dedicated to St. Aldhelm, first bishop of Sherborne. Its central turret,

SECTION 24
WORTH MALTRAVERS to POOLE HARBOUR

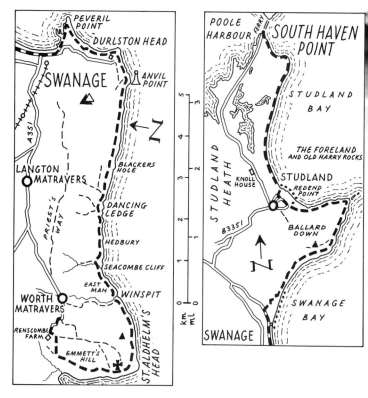

which may have held a light, and its headland location suggest a secondary role as a navigation beacon for shipping. A short scramble down from the Coastguard lookout to a ledge reveals a chaos of rocks and vegetation, including a conspicuous pillar left standing by the quarrymen.

(A more direct route from Worth Matravers to St. Aldhelm's Head follows the stony, pot-holed track (vehicles not allowed to the end) directly south from Renscombe Farm, but it is rather dull for walking on.)

A stone marker indicates the way forward past the Coastguard look-out and derelict wartime wireless telegraph installations. Views have opened up ahead over the Isle of Purbeck, this south-eastern corner of Dorset, and along the much quarried limestone cliffs.

In a mile of walking accompanied by the call of seabirds, you approach **WINSPIT** disused quarry and may notice signs of terracing on the steep valley slopes. These medieval strip lynchets are thought to have been used for emergency cereal cultivation when older local soils became infertile, or to bolster supplies to feed an expanding population. Winspit was producing stone until the mid-1940's and it is possible to explore some of the labyrinthine workings from which came the famous Purbeck Portland Limestone. (As in all quarries, care is needed to avoid accidents - the rock faces and galleries can be dangerously unstable.)

There are some big caves here too, and a memorial tablet to Ian Campbell Johnstone who 'loved birds and green places and the wind on the heath'. Windspit is the westernmost site of the spider-orchid, emblem of the Dorset Naturalists' Trust.

You cross a stream (path left to Worth Matravers - 1 mile) and resume clifftop walking above quarry galleries and outside a field fence. East Man denotes the unceremonious mass grave of 168 passengers from the East Indiaman 'Halsewell', wrecked here in January 1786: only 80 survived. Before the Rev. Gryll's act of 1808 which allowed bodies proper burial in consecrated ground, wreck victims were interred where they washed ashore in case they were heathen.

With Anvil Point lighthouse now not far ahead, you pass between quarry workings and the sea and farther on reach another quarry at **SEACOMBE CLIFF,** where a short inland diversion avoids the sheer rock face (track left to Worth Matravers). About 800m on lies the next quarry - unnamed on maps but known by climbers as Hedbury. With caves and a Napoleonic cannon mounted on a ledge, its other name is Cannon Cove.

A fence to seaward affords some security on these high and wild clifftops. Before long, **DANCING LEDGE** appears below - a popular summer picnic destination for the more adventurous and reached by footpath from Langton Matravers just to the west of Swanage. The roughly hewn, seaweedy swimming pool was cut in the rock ledges in 1893 for boys of Durnford House School. Visible across Dancing Ledge are cart tracks, worn into the surface during the loading of stone onto waiting ketches.

NOTE: Many paths and tracks link Worth Matravers with the coast between Chapman's Pool and Dancing Ledge. They are well signed and cleared, enabling good circular routes to be devised. Additionally, the Priest's Way (of Saxon origin) connects Worth with Swanage and offers an alternative to the coast path or part of a larger circuit.

Several parallel trods across mainly rough pasture lead on, but there is little chance of going astray. The tall pylons beyond Blacker's Hole are used in conjunction with another pair inland past the lighthouse to measure an exact nautical mile (6,080ft. - 1,853m) in warship speed trials.

As is invariably the case when approaching a centre of population, paths are increasingly well used. You soon enter Durlston Country Park which attempts to reconcile public access and the protection of wildlife habitats. The lighthouse on **ANVIL POINT** is also a Mountain Rescue Post for sea cliff climbers (open weekday afternoons).

The coast path comes round seaward of the lighthouse, drops over a dry valley and enters a delightful stony track, walled above sheer cliff ledges with their myriad seabirds. You will pass the entrance to Tilly Whim Caves, 102ft. (31m) above sea level. Originally a quarry created in 1887 by a Mr. Tilly, who used a 'whim' (a horse-drawn winch), the caves are now closed to the public owing to rock falls.

There are observation bays with bird identification charts on **DURL-STON HEAD,** and just down to the right stands the Great Globe, 10ft. (3m) in diameter and weighing 40 tons. This Portland stone curiosity was commissioned in the 1890's by George Burt, a Swanage eccentric who also built the clifftop Durlston Castle.

Forking left, the coast path climbs alongside old City of London bollards (brought back by ships delivering stone there) and passes the Globe Head cafe/gift shop *(open 10.00am. to 4.00pm. in the season)* near a large stone chart of the English Channel. Farther up on the high wall of Durlston Castle is more 'educational' stonemasonry, installed presumably for the edification of trippers!

The Castle offers bars, meals and snacks. From here, fork right uphill, past a car park *(Information Centre nearby - details of circular*

Swanage

walks, etc.) and continue along a wooded carriage drive - Isle of Wight Road - provided with occasional viewing bays. Eventually you cross a footbridge and climb steps past flats to Belle Vue Road. Turn right, then right again at a bend with bollards to gain grassy clifftops overlooking Swanage Bay. Old Harry Rocks and the Isle of Wight are visible in good weather - a momentous view indeed for long-distance walkers, for whom the South West Way (or its easternmost stage) will soon end.

The cliffs are dangerously unstable but can be avoided on the easy descent to the Coastguard lookout and lifeboat station on **PEVERIL POINT**. However, you are soon forced by high tide up from the foreshore to a car park and along a tarmac lane, views spoiled by recent building. An alternative descent stays on the grassy down and makes directly for roadside parking above the harbour pier at **SWANAGE** *(all shops, services and accommodation, including youth hostel; buses; museum; boat trips; Swanage Steam Railway - open daily in August, weekends in July and September, Sundays only in May and June; car parks; early closing Thursday)*.

A sizeable and mostly modern resort, Swanage owes its popularity to the coming of the railways in the 19th century which, fortuitously coincided with the decline of its quarry industry. The long beach of fine sand and pebbles is flanked by a promenade with all the usual amenities close by. The bay was formed by marine erosion of soft

185

Wealden Beds.

Walk all the way along Swanage promenade to Ocean Bay Stores where the road veers inland. By far the best onward route, tide permitting, is to continue on the pedestrian promenade past beach huts and refreshment booths. Private steps up left serve this 500m stretch of popular sandy beach, but the cliff is unstable towards the far end. Take to the beach there and just before the last wooden groyne, turn left up steps by a stream (Shep's Hollow) to meet the coast path at a marker stone on low cliffs.

If the tide is high, walk up Ulwell Road from Ocean Bay Stores and fork right past the church. Another right turn into Ballard Road leads to the private Ballard Estate, site of a 1st World War army camp. Go into the estate, fork right in 150m, turn left then right out between bungalows onto grassy clifftops. Turn left and in a short distance you meet the beach route just past the stream footbridge.

The well walked path winds along field edges, finally mounting the chalk ridge of Ballard Cliff, with superb retrospective views over Swanage Bay. The summit is marked by a trig. pillar. Ballard Down forms the eastern end of the Purbeck Hills, originally connected to the Isle of Wight some 8,000 years ago. Typical chalk downland plants which disappeared during wartime cereal cultivation have been reintroduced and the area is designated a Site of Special Scientific Interest.

Descending gently, a mile's walking outside a field fence and above vertical cliffs bring you to **THE FORELAND** and the much photographed Old Harry Rocks, an assortment of chalk stacks which are slowly succumbing to the waves. This is a fitting last viewpoint for eastbound walkers who will be gazing for the first time at a coastline ahead no longer belonging to the South West Way.

Turning west, you pass through a small wood and follow the clear track down to the road near toilets at South Beach, **STUDLAND** *(pub; shop; seasonal beach cafes; accommodation; buses for Swanage and Bournemouth: telephone; car parks; toilets; early closing Thursday)*. The Norman church and adjacent old buildings are worth looking at.

Waymarking is poor in the village. At low tide you can turn sharp right to South Beach and walk round Redend Point. Otherwise go through the village and turn right by the National Trust's Manor House Hotel on a path to the beach.

STUDLAND HEATH is a 400-acre National Nature Reserve containing flora and fauna of exceptional variety. It was set up in 1962 to protect the rare sand lizard and smooth snake and a nature trail has been established, its entrance at Knoll House a mile north of Studland

The Sandbanks Chain Ferry, Poole Harbour

on the Sandbanks toll road. In stark contrast to most of the South West Way where wind and waves are eating back the land, here deposition is at work. Visitors are warned about the considerable fire risk, witness the diamong-shaped Fire Rendezvous Point notices in the reserve.

Walking along the sands of Studland Bay, you may have to avert your eyes on the middle part of this vast beach as it is used by naturists: in hot weather, on the other hand, you may be tempted to join them! In Shell Bay there are warnings about unexploded ammunition and phosphorous (resembling rock) at the waterline which can burn.

All being well, you will survive the 3½ miles (6km) sand bash and emerge on the toll road from Studland at **SOUTH HAVEN POINT** *(cafe/beach shop; telephone; buses for Swanage and Bournemouth; car park; toilets).* For the terminus of Britain's longest official footpath, it is a rather inauspicious place, busy in summer with traffic (buses have priority!) queuing for the chain ferry to Sandbanks on Poole Harbour. It runs every 20 minutes daily (more frequently at peak periods) from early morning to 11.00pm., all year round except 2 weeks in November. Frequent buses connect with central **POOLE and BOURNE-MOUTH** *(all shops, services and accommodation; Tourist Information; British Rail and coach stations; etc.)*

If the urge to continue walking is irresistable, the Bournemouth coast path runs east from Sandbanks to Milford-on-Sea - a distance of 20 miles (32km). Here you could pick up the Solent Way for a further 60 miles (97km) to Emsworth, north of Hayling Island.

USEFUL ADDRESSES AND TELEPHONE NUMBERS

AIRPORTS:
Bodmin Airport, tel. Cardinham (020 882) 463
British International Helicopters, tel. Penzance (0736) 63871
Brymon Airways, tel. Newquay (063 73) 860551 or
                      Plymouth (0752) 707023
Exeter Airport, tel. Exeter (0392) 67433
Land's End St. Just Airport, tel. Penzance (0736) 787017

BRITISH RAIL PASSENGER INFORMATION:
Exeter (0392) 33551
Penzance (0736) 65831
Plymouth (0752) 221300

BRITISH TOURIST AUTHORITY:
Information Centre, 64 St. James' Street, London SW1

BRITISH TRUST FOR CONSERVATION VOLUNTEERS:
36 St. Mary's Street, Wallingford, Oxon. OX10 0EU, tel. (0491) 39766

CAMPING AND CARAVANNING CLUB:
11 Grosvenor Place, London SW1W 0EX

COUNTRYSIDE COMMISSION:
John Dower House, Crescent Place, Cheltenham, Glos. GL50 3RA
  tel. (0242) 521381

FERRIES:
Helford River - Ferry Boat Inn, Helford Passage, Nr. Falmouth,
  tel. Falmouth (0326) 250 278
Falmouth/St. Mawes - St. Mawes Ferry Co., Ambergate, 14 Rame Croft,
  Rame, Nr. Penryn, tel. (0209) 861020
Fowey to Polruan - Polruan Ferry Co. Ltd., Fowey, Cornwall,
  tel. Fowey (072 683) 2626
Cremyll to Plymouth - Tamar Cruising and Cremyll Ferry, Penhellis,
  Maker Lane, Millbrook, Torpoint, Cornwall, tel. Plymouth (0752) 822105
River Yealm - P.J.Carter, Futtocks End, The Green, Newton Ferrers,
  tel. Plymouth (0752) 872189
Bigbury to Bantham (River Avon) H.Cater, Yorick, West Buckland,
  Kingsbridge, Devon, tel. Kingsbridge (0548) 560593
Salcombe to East Portlemouth - The Salcombe Ferry Operating Co. Ltd.,
  Landmark House, Landmark Road, Salcombe, Devon,
  tel. Salcombe (054 884) 2863 or 2061
Dartmouth to Kingswear - South Hams District Council, Ferry Manager's
  Dept., The Square, Kingswear, Dartmouth, tel. Kingswear (080 425) 342

Shaldon to Teignmouth - Teignbridge District Council Tourism Dept., Seafront, Teignmouth, tel. Teignmouth (062 67) 79770

Starcross to Exmouth - Mr. B.Rackley, Starcross Pier and Pleasure Co., 26 Marine Parade, Dawlish, tel. Dawlish (0626) 862452

Studland to Sandbanks (Poole Harbour) - Bournemouth-Swanage Motor Road and Ferry Co., Floating Bridge, Sandbanks, Poole, tel. Studland (092 944) 203

FRIENDS OF THE EARTH:
377 City Road, London EC1V 1NA, tel. (01) 837 0731

HOSPITALS (with Casualty Dept.):
Truro City Hospital, tel. (0872) 74242
West Cornwall Hospital, Penzance, tel. (0736) 62382
Weymouth and District Hospital, tel. (0305) 972211

LONG DISTANCE WALKERS ASSOCIATION:
11 Thorn Bank, Onslow Village, Guildford, Surrey GU2 5PL; (handbook £5.95 post free)

LULWORTH RANGES:
tel. (0929) 462721 ext. 819 (office hours) or ext. 824

NATIONAL TRUST:
36 Queen Anne's Gate, London SW1H 9AS, tel. (01) 222 9251
Regional Information Offices:-
for Dorset - Dorset & Somerset Regional Information Office, Stourton, Warminster, Wilts. BA12 6QD, tel. (0747) 840560
for Devon - Devon Information Office, Killerton House, Broadclyst, Exeter, Devon EX5 3LE, tel. (0392) 881691
for Cornwall - Cornwall Information Office, The Estate Office, Lanhydrock Park, Bodmin, Cornwall PL30 4DE, tel. (0208) 4281

NATURE CONSERVANCY COUNCIL:
Northminister House, Northminster Road, Peterborough, Cambs. PE1 1UA tel. (0733) 40345
for South West Region - Roughmoor, Bishop's Hull, Taunton, Somerset TA1 5AA, tel. (0823) 83211

RAMBLERS ASSOCIATION:
1/5 Wandsworth Road, London SW8 2LJ

ROYAL SOCIETY FOR THE PROTECTION OF BIRDS:
The Lodge, Sandy, Beds. SG19 2DL, tel. (0767) 80551

SOUTH WEST WAY ASSOCIATION:
Membership Secretary, 1 Orchard Drive, Kingskerswell, Newton Abbot, Devon TQ12 5DG, tel. (080 47) 3061

MAIN TOURIST INFORMATION CENTRES:
Penzance - Station Road, tel. (0736) 62207/62341
Falmouth - Town Hall, The Moor, tel. (0326) 312300
Fowey - The Post Office, Custom House Hill, tel. (072 683) 3616

Looe - Guildhall, Fore Street, tel. (050 36) 2072
Plymouth - Devon Civic Centre, tel. (0752) 264849/51
Salcombe - Main Road, tel. (054 884) 2736
Torbay - Torbay Tourist Board, Torquay, tel. (0803) 211211
Exmouth - Alexandra Terrace, tel. (0395) 263744
Beer & Seaton - Publicity Office, Seaton
Weymouth - Pavilion Complex, Esplanade, tel. (0305) 772444
Poole - Poole Quay, tel. (0202) 673322

WEATHER FORECASTS:
tel. (0898) 500481

WEST COUNTRY TOURIST BOARD:
Trinity Court, 37 Southernhay East, Exeter EX1 1QN, tel. (0392) 76351

WESTERN NATIONAL BUSES:
National House, Queen Street, Exeter, Devon EX4 3TF

YOUTH HOSTELS: (in walk order)
Castle Horneck, Alverton, Penzance TR19 7NT, tel. (0736) 62666
Parc Behan, School Hill, Coverack TR12 6SA, tel. (0326) 280583
Pendennis Castle, Falmouth TR11 4LP, tel. (0326) 311435
Boswinger, Gorran, St. Austell PL26 6LL, tel. (0726) 843514
Belmont Place, Devenport Road, Stoke, Plymouth, tel. (0752) 562189
Overbecks, Sharpitor, Salcombe TQ8 8LW, tel. (054 884) 2856
Maypool, Galmpton, Brixham TQ5 0ET, tel. (0803) 842444
Bovey Combe, Townsend, Beer EX12 3LL, tel. (0297) 20296
West Rivers House, West Allington, Bridport DT6 5BW, tel. (0308) 22655
Litton Cheney, Dorchester DT2 9AT, tel. (030 83) 340
School Lane, West Lulworth BH20 5SA, tel. (092 941) 564
Cluny, Cluny Crescent, Swanage BH19 2BS, tel. (0929) 422113

BIBLIOGRAPHY

Coastline - Britain's Threatened Heritage by Greenpeace (Kingfisher Books)

Cornwall's Structure and Scenery' by R.M.Barton (Tor Mark Press

The Making of the English Landscape by W.G. Hoskins (Pelican)

The AA Book of the Seaside

Cornish Shipwrecks - The South Coast by C.Carter (Pan Books)

Flowers of the Cornish Coast by J.A.Paton (Tor Mark Press)

Hallsands - A Pictorial History by K.Tanner & P. Walsh

South West Way handbook by the SWWA (Devon Books)

A Guide to the Isle of Purbeck by Chris Jesty (Dovecote Press)

The West Country Beach Guide by Andrew Carless (Garnett Press)

The National Trust Guide to the Coast by Tony Soper (Webb and Bower)

A COAST PATH CODE

Beware crumbling and unstable cliff edges at all times.

Ensure the tide is favourable before beach-walking beneath cliffs.

If walking alone, leave details of your itinerary with a responsible person.

Keep to the coast path or other definitive rights of way over farmland.

Observe notices and waymarks, especially through M.O.D. property and over private land.

Respect hedges, walls and fences by only crossing them at gates and stiles.

Never pitch a tent on farmland without first obtaining permission to do so. Avoid damaging plants, trees and growing crops.

Respect the privacy of inhabitants living close to the path.

Keep dogs under close control near livestock.

Take your litter with you.

If you see anyone in difficulties on land or at sea, dial 999 from the nearest telephone and ask for the Coastguard. Being able to give a map grid reference or other accurate positional reference for the incident is of great value to the rescue services.

If you need assistance yourself, the international distress call is 6 long signals (eg. whistle blasts, shouts, torch flashes etc.), repeated at 1-minute intervals. The reply is 3 signals at 1-minute intervals.

A SEA-BATHING CODE

Where possible, bathe within areas patrolled by lifeguards.

Only bathe between the 2 red and yellow flags. Red flags denote danger.

Keep a careful eye on children and non-swimmers - even quite shallow water can be dangerous.

Don't bathe in areas marked by black and white chequered flags - these are for malibu surfboards and canoes only.

Never use inflatables on exposed coastlines and in offshore winds.

Avoid bathing directly after a meal.

Avoid bathing at least one hour each side of low tide or in a heavy swell on unsupervised beaches.

Keep a watchful eye on the state of the tide if bathing beneath high cliffs or in river estuaries.

DISTANCE TABLE (including major variants.
Approximate mileages rounded up or down.)

SECTION	FROM	TO	ML	KM	ACCUMMULATIVE ML	ACCUMMULATIVE KM
1	PENZANCE	Marazion	3	5	3	5
	Marazion	Praa Sands	6	10	9	15
	Praa Sands	PORTHLEVEN	4	6	13	21
2	PORTHLEVEN	Mullion Cove	7	12	20	32
	Mullion Cove	LIZARD	6	10	26	42
3	LIZARD	Cadgwith	3	5	29	47
	Cadgwith	Coverack	6	10	35	56
	Coverack	PORTHALLOW	5	8	40	64
4	PORTHALLOW	Helford	6	10	46	74
	Helford	Maenporth	6	10	52	84
	Maenporth	FALMOUTH	3	5	55	89
5	FALMOUTH	PORTSCATHO via ferry to Place	6	10	61	98
6	PORTSCATHO	Nare Head	5	8	66	106
	Nare Head	Portloe	2	3	68	109
	Portloe	Dodman Point	6	10	74	119
	Dodman Point	GORRAN HAVEN	2	3	76	122
7	GORRAN HAVEN	Mevagissey	3	5	79	127
	Mevagissey	Charlestown	6	10	85	137
	Charlestown	PAR	4	6	89	143
8	PAR	Fowey	5	8	94	151
	Fowey	Polperro	6	10	100	161
	Polperro	LOOE	5	8	105	169
9	LOOE	Downderry	4	6	109	175
	Downderry	Freathy	6	10	115	185
	Freathy	Rame Head	3	5	118	190
	Rame Head	Kingsand	3	5	121	195
	Freathy	Kingsand via short-cut	4	6		
	Kingsand	PLYMOUTH (Cremyll ferry)	3	5	124	200

					ACCUMMULATIVE	
SECTION	FROM	TO	ML	KM	ML	KM
10	PLYMOUTH (Turnchapel)	NOSS MAYO via River Yealm ferry	8	13	132	212
11	NOSS MAYO	River Erme	9	14	141	227
	River Erme	BIGBURY-ON-SEA	4	6	145	233
12	BIGBURY-ON-SEA	Hope Cove	6	10	151	243
	Hope Cove	Bolberry Down	2	3	153	246
	Bolberry Down	SALCOMBE	5	8	158	254
13	SALCOMBE	Start Point	8	13	166	267
	Start Point	Torcross	3	5	169	272
	Torcross	STOKE FLEMING	5	8	174	280
14	STOKE FLEMING	Dartmouth	4	6	178	286
	Dartmouth	Man Sands	7	11	185	298
	Man Sands	BRIXHAM	4	6	189	304
15	BRIXHAM	TORQUAY HARBOUR	8	13	197	317
16	TORQUAY HARBOUR	Shaldon	9	14	206	332
	Shaldon	Dawlish	3	5	209	336
	Dawlish	EXMOUTH via Starcross ferry	4	6	213	343
17	EXMOUTH	Budleigh Salterton	5	8	218	351
	Budleigh Salterton	Ladram Bay	4	6	222	357
	Ladram Bay	SIDMOUTH	3	5	225	362
18	SIDMOUTH	Branscombe Mouth	6	10	231	372
	Branscombe Mouth	SEATON	3	5	234	377
19	SEATON	Lyme Regis	6	10	240	386
	Lyme Regis	Charmouth via new path	3	5	243	391
	Charmouth	SEATOWN	4	6	247	397
20	SEATOWN	West Bay	3	5	250	402
	West Bay	West Bexington	6	10	256	412
	West Bexington	ABBOTSBURY	3	5	259	417

SECTION	FROM	TO	ML	KM	ACCUMMULATIVE ML	KM
21	ABBOTSBURY East Fleet	East Fleet WEYMOUTH via Portland Harbour	7	11	266	428
			7	11	273	439
	WEYMOUTH	Osmington Mills	5	8	278	447
22	West Bexington	Osmington Mills via Dorset Ridgeway	16	26	variant	
	Osmington Mills Durdle Door	Durdle Door LULWORTH COVE	5	8	283	455
			1	2	284	457
23	LULWORTH COVE Worbarrow Tout	Worbarrow Tout Kimmeridge (Gaulter Gap) WORTH MATRAVERS	4	6	288	463
			3	5	291	468
	Kimmeridge		5	8	296	476
24	WORTH MATRAVERS St.Aldhelm's Head Swanage	St.Aldhelm's Head Swanage POOLE HARBOUR (South Haven Point)	2	3	298	480
			7	11	305	491
			7	11	312	502

CICERONE PRESS GUIDES

Cicerone publish a range of reliable guides to walking and climbing in Europe

FRANCE
TOUR OF MONT BLANC
CHAMONIX MONT BLANC - A Walking Guide
TOUR OF THE OISANS: GR54
WALKING THE FRENCH ALPS: GR5
THE CORSICAN HIGH LEVEL ROUTE: GR20
ROCK CLIMBS IN THE VERDON
THE WAY OF ST. JAMES: GR65

FRANCE/SPAIN
WALKS & CLIMBS IN THE PYRENEES

SPAIN
WALKING IN MALLORCA
WALKS & CLIMBS IN THE PICOS DE EUROPA

FRANCE/SWITZERLAND
THE JURA - Walking the High Route and Winter Ski Traverses

SWITZERLAND
WALKS IN THE ENGADINE
THE VALAIS - A Walking Guide

GERMANY/AUSTRIA
THE KALKALPEN TRAVERSE
KLETTERSTEIG - Scrambles in the Northern Limestone Alps
MOUNTAIN WALKING IN AUSTRIA
WALKING IN THE SALZKAMMERGUT
KING LUDWIG WAY

ITALY
ALTA VIA - High Level Walks in the Dolomites
VIA FERRATA - Scrambles in the Dolomites
ITALIAN ROCK - Selected Rock Climbs in Northern Italy
CLASSIC CLIMBS IN THE DOLOMITES

OTHER AREAS
THE MOUNTAINS OF GREECE - A Walker's Guide
TREKS & CLIMBS in the mountains of Rhum and Petra, JORDAN
CRETE: OFF THE BEATEN TRACK
ATLAS MOUNTAINS

GENERAL OUTDOOR BOOKS
LANDSCAPE PHOTOGRAPHY
FIRST AID FOR HILLWALKERS
MOUNTAIN WEATHER
JOURNEY AFTER DAWN
MOUNTAINEERING LITERATURE
SKI THE NORDIC WAY- A Manual of Cross-Country Skiing
THE ADVENTURE ALTERNATIVE

CANOEING
SNOWDONIA WILD WATER, SEA & SURF
WILDWATER CANOEING

CARTOON BOOKS
ON FOOT & FINGER
ON MORE FEET & FINGERS
LAUGHS ALONG THE PENNINE WAY

CICERONE PRESS

Also a full range of guide-books to walking, scrambling, ice-climbing, rock climbing, and other adventurous pursuits in Britain and abroad.

Other guides are constantly being added to the Cicerone List. Available from bookshops, outdoor equipment shops of direct (send for price list) from CICERONE PRESS, 2 POLICE SQUARE, MILNTHORPE CUMBRIA LA7 7PY

PRINTED BY MARTIN'S OF BERWICK

Back Endpaper: The Cobb, Lyme Regis.
Golden Cap top left